ARTHUR AND THE BRITONS
IN HISTORY AND ANCIENT POETRY

auty tabian · hitt attad y
daeth tad byulaun · llat
byndur tra meffury bu
ynan · llas haelon odin
on tra uuan · Dby uir ·
nod maur eu clod · gan ·
elgan · Ciroy· Dbuy a th
uit · Ruy · a Ruy · uav a th
rau imdoeth y doethan ·

A page from the Black Book of Carmarthen.

ARTHUR AND THE BRITONS IN HISTORY AND ANCIENT POETRY

by
W F SKENE
edited by
Derek Bryce

Taken from the
Four Ancient Books
of Wales
by W F Skene
Edinburgh 1868.

Published in 1987 by Llanerch Enterprises
Llanerch, Felinfach, Lampeter, Dyfed.
SA48 8PJ.

ISBN 0947992111

GAEFRAN

ARGOED LLWYFAIN

LLWYFENYDD or LINNIUS

CLAS FFICHTI

Styrlyn

Caer Eidyn

REGED or MURIEFF

Carron

CATRAETH

Bouden Hill

Alclyde

Ardunin Dindir

y Mur

MANAU Brithwy

ARECLUTA

Caer Clut

GODDEU

Coet Boit

R. Clyde

CANAWON

R. Irvine

Glein

Glein

ARFYNYD

MYNYW

Firth of Clyde

Dundevenel

Bretrwn

COEL

CYMRY

R. Doon

Caer Caradawg

Bryn Carrwg

Gorvan

CARRAWG

Caer Brug

R. Nie

Penend Cludwin

NOVANT

Caer Rheon

Loch Ruin

Torra

GALWYDDEL Peithwyr

R. Nie

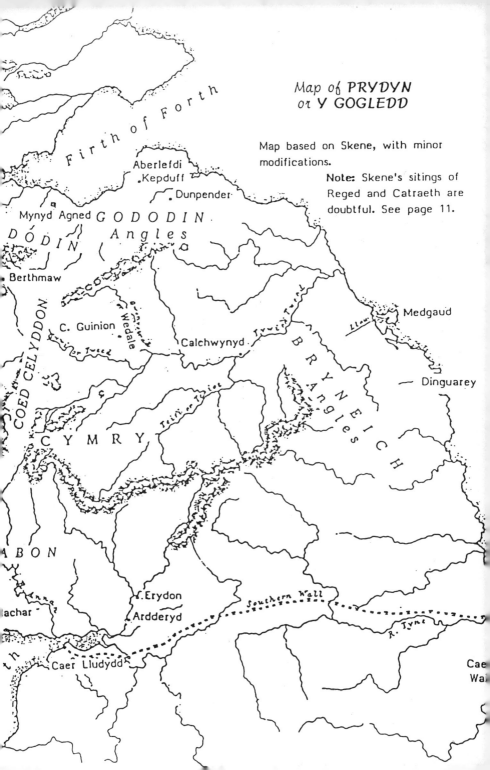

Note chapters 2, 3, and 4 are from W. F. Skene, 'The Four Ancient Books of Wales.' Introduction and notes are by the editor.

INTRODUCTION.

This book contains an account of the period of early British history, from the decline of Roman power, until the second half of the sixth century. Taken from Skene's 'Four Ancient Books of Wales,' it includes his chapters on the history of the period, and translations of ancient poems.

In order to understand something about the poems from the Ancient Books of Wales, it is necessary to take a look at the history of Britain during the period to which they relate.

The Roman province extended to the northern wall, a defensive earthwork between the Firth of Forth and the Clyde; it was constructed to keep out the Picts, or painted men, whom the Cymry, or Welsh-speaking Britons called the Ffichti, and also the Brithwyr, meaning the speckled or spotted men. The Romans also constructed a second line of defence, a southern wall - Hadrian's wall - from the Tyne to the Solway Firth.

Between the late fourth and early fifth century, the 'Barbarians from the North' broke through the northern defences. These barbarians were the Picts, accompanied by Scots from Ireland who had settled on their western shores, and possibly also Saxons who had done likewise in the east of their territory. On the first two occasions, the Romans sent military assistance to push the invaders back and repair the northern defences; but on the third occasion the Romans advised the Britons to look to their own defence.

The last Roman legions in Britain seem to have been deployed mainly in the defence of the northern wall, and also the north eastern shores where there was a risk of invasion by marauding Saxons. It would be reasonable to assume that the

Britons on being told to defend themselves, set up an organzation after the Roman model.

The Roman legions in Britain had, on occasion, elected 'Imperatores,' Maximus and Constantine for example, whom the Britons must have seen functioning as military commanders-in-chief for the defence of the country. The Britons appear to have selected such a leader from amongst themselves, not so much as King of all the British, but as commander-in-chief of the combined British resistance. In the old Welsh texts this leader is given the title of Gwledig, which means chieftain in Welsh, and which is often given the Anglicized spelling of Guledig. Some of the old Welsh texts referred to the Roman leaders in the same way, for example, Maxim Gwledig. In the old Latin texts the Guledig seems variously referred to as Cunedda, Ambrosius, or Dux, but never Rex or King.

After the collapse of Roman power in Britain, and the barbarian invasion from the North, the Saxons successfully invaded much of East, and South-eastern Britain, and the Scots from Ireland seem to have occupied much of the western half of Wales. This left the Britons in the South-west, and the Cymry, or Welsh-speaking Britons in two areas, Wales and adjacent parts of England, and an extended Cumbria in the North.

The first appearance of a British military commander-in-chief, or Guledig, would seem to be Cunedda, who, abandoning the defence of the North, retreated to Wales where he and his sons or descendants drove the Scots out of the land, returning the whole of Wales to the Cymry.

The next appearance of a Guledig, is that of Ambrosius Aurelianus, followed by Arthur. Many who have written about Arthur as a historical leader, have seen his main campaign as directed against the West Saxons, with a final great battle which established peace, at Badon Hill, near Bath. Skene, however, took the view that such a site was too far west for a major battle to be fought between Arthur and the West Saxons. Skene took the view that Arthur's campaign of great battles took place in the North, beyond Hadrian's wall, and aimed at recovering the territories of the Northern Cymry and securing their defences. In this one campaign, Skene claims that Arthur was able to defeat both the Picts and the Northern Saxons. In conducting his campaign in the North, Arthur, as Guledig, a title inherited from the Roman model, would have been continuing the Roman policy that defence of the North was vital for the country as a whole.

In support of his view of a northern Arthurian campaign, Skene points out that many of the old Welsh texts refer to Prydyn, and the Men of the North. Prydyn was the name given by the Welsh-speaking Britons to the lands between the walls, the region of Strathclyde; Prydain, on the other hand, was the land of the South Cymry, Wales and the adjacent parts of England. Skene also points out that a campaign in the North would explain why there are no references to Arthur and his battles in the Anglo-Saxon Chronicle, which refers mainly to events south of the Humber.

Of those who have written on Arthurian history, few have taken great note of Skene's veiws. One reason for this is that we all start off with a simplified picture from elementary history books, learnt at an early age, of the Britons being pushed westwards by the Saxons, into Wales and Cornwall, and we tend to assume without question that any decisive battle between the Britons and

the Saxons *must* have taken place somewhere
east, or south-east, of Wales. Another problem is
that many writers on the subject have not spoken
Welsh, and have tended to make greater use of
the Latin histories than the old Welsh texts.

One of the questions that arises from Skene's
view, is: If Arthur's great battles were in the
North, how did they establish a peace between
the Saxons and the Britons in the South? A pos-
sible answer is that the West Saxons had become
settled and were farming their land, and that any
future pressure for Saxon territorial expansion
was more likely to come from new immigrants
from the Continent, young warriors who, taking
the short sea route, may often have landed in
Scotland. Futhermore, a great defeat of the Picts
and the Saxons in the North could have enhanced
Arthur's reputation to such an extent that the
West Saxons may have preferred peace rather
than risk an encounter with him. This, however,
cannot be established on the historical evidence,
and the question posed above exposes the weaker
side of Skene's theory.

A final objection to Skene's argument is that
he himself was a Scot! Although this is not an
intelligent criticism, such a thought may occur to
many who have noticed how French writers try
to place as much of the Arthurian Saga as they
can in Armorican Brittany, how Cornish tradition
places the Battle of Camlan at Slaughter Bridge
near Tintagel, and how many English writers have
favoured Badon Hill near Bath as the site for
Arthur's great victory. Many will no doubt agree
with Skene that some of Arthur's battles were
fought in the North, but most will still favour a
southern location for his greatest battle, and the
Cornish one for his last.

Skene provided a map of Prydyn, or Y Gogledd, the Northern Territories beyond Hadrian's wall. It is reproduced in this book. One of Skene's modern critics, Sir Ifor Williams, has agreed that he is probably right in his identification of some of the fortified sites, such as Carridon, near Bo'Ness on the Forth, being the Caer Eidyn of the ancient Welsh texts. Williams thinks Edinburgh, Skene's Mynyd Agned, relates more with Ysgor Eidyn than with Din Eidyn; he also considers that Cattraeth in the old texts refers to Catterick in Yorkshire, and not to Skene's site near Edinburgh. Sir Ifor considers that Reged (or Rheged) is shown too small on Skene's map; he considers this territory to have extended further south, at least as far as Carlisle, and possibly even into Lancashire. It is doubtful if anyone will ever write the last word on the history of those times, and what we can say of Skene is that his argument represents an important contribution to the Arthurian debate. Like many other contributions, it can be seen as containing a measure of truth, but not the total truth.

The poems contained in this book, referring to Arthur, and early British history, are from the Ancient Books of Wales. The Four Ancient Books are: The Black Book of Carmarthen, the Book of Aneurin, the Book of Taliesin, and the Red Book of Hergest. According to tradition, these books were written by four Bards in the sixth century, namely Myrddin, Aneurin, Taliesin, and Llwyarch Hen. The surviving manuscripts of these books date from the twelfth to the fifteenth centuries. There are many passages in them which quite clearly refer to events later than the sixth century. They also include interpolated material, such as theological passages which may have been inserted by monks to protect themselves from being criticized for transcribing non-Christian works. We should think, therefore, that the Book of Taliesin, for example, contains poems 'in the Style,' or 'of the School of Taliesin,' and so on.

Of the poems translated in this book, the first section contains those which Skene considered to bear the mark of antiquity. The poems were translated for Skene by the Rev. Robert Williams. They were published in 1868, before the foundations of modern Welsh scholarship had been laid down. In view of this, the reader might well ask why we have not replaced them by the translations of Dr. Gwenogvryn Evans, for example.

It is true that, for these books, the foundations of modern Welsh scholarship were laid down by Dr. Evans, and that he established near-definitive Welsh texts based on studies of the surviving manuscripts. His Welsh texts are still used by scholars today, with only minor modifications. However, when Dr. Evans prepared his poems for publication, he amended them by inserting words in italics which he thought were missing from the old manuscripts; then he translated his amended texts into English. Had his amendments been purely logical, they might have been accepted as passable by all but the extreme purists, but he had included insertions which many now consider to be illogical, and based on a false historical view of the books. He had convinced himself that the works were not ancient, because they were largely written in the Welsh of Norman times. This can be compared perhaps with a historian of the future looking at an edition of Chaucer in modern English, and concluding from the style of writing that Chaucer could not date from before the nineteenth century! To give a single example let us look at a poem usually called the Spoils of Annwn, from the Book of Taliesin, one which Skene included amongst those he considered to have the mark of antiquity. This poem speaks of Arthur in his mythological, rather than historical role. It tells of a raid on Annwn, the Celtic 'other-world.' Arthur leads the raid in his ship Prydwen, and only seven of the raiders return home alive. Most Welsh scholars, including Sir Ifor Williams, have considered this poem to be ancient, and yet Evans was so convinced that it belonged to the time of the Third Crusade that he changed the title to 'King Richard at Joppa and Acre,' and he interpolated the name of Saladin, who was King Richard's opponent, in the middle of the text! Commenting on this kind of unwarranted alteration, Sir Ifor Williams said that it is impossible to take him seriously, and that it is incredible that a scholar should treat the old texts in this preposterous manner. That is why we have retained the old translations in this book. Those who wish to read a modern introduction to the Ancient Books are referred to 'The Beginnings of Welsh Poetry' by Sir Ifor Williams (University of Wales Press).

To complete this introduction, we should now return to Skene's view of King Arthur's campaign as re-establishing the Cymric kingdoms in the southern half of Scotland. According to Skene, the Men of the North soon lapsed into Paganism; they made an unholy alliance with the Picts and Saxons which resulted in the defeat of Arthur and the Christian Cymry from the South, at the battle of Camlan. From that time on, the Cymry in the North became more isolated from those of the South, in Wales. The Cymric kingdoms seem to have survived in the North with varying fortunes

until the year 890. One of the copies of the Brut
y Tywysogion, an old Welsh text, has the following entry for that year:

> "The men of Strathclyde who would not
> unite with the Saxons were obliged to
> leave their country and go to Gwynned,
> and Anarawd (King of Wales) gave them
> leave to inhabit the country taken from
> him by the Saxons, comprising Maelor,
> the Vale of Clwyd, Rhyvoniog, and Teg-
> eingl, if they could drive the Saxons out,
> which they did bravely. And the Saxons
> came on that account a second time
> against Anarawd, and fought the action
> of Cymryd, in which the Cymry con-
> quered the Saxons and drove them whol-
> ly out of the country; and so Gwynned
> was freed from the Saxons by the might
> of the Gwyr y Gogledd or Men of the
> North."

If the above is true, it would help to explain
why the Four Ancient Books of Wales contain so
many references to Prydyn and the Men of the
North, for the latter would have returned to
Wales bringing their oral or written traditions
with them. Prior to the Dissolution, the old books
seem to have been transcribed, and kept in the
monasteries of Wales, but after, they were sought
out by private collectors thanks to whom many
have survived and found their way into permanent
collections.

We now end this introduction, which is followed by Skene's account of early history, and
the poems. We apologise for any repetition which
the reader might find, but we are of the opinion
that Skene's chapters will be easier to follow if
one has had a preview of what they are about.

CHAPTER 2.

SOURCES OF THE EARLY HISTORY OF WALES.

In order to discriminate between what is true and what is fabulous in the early history of Wales as presented to us in the historic literature subsequent to the twelfth century, and to disentangle the fragments of real history contained in them, so as to enable us to form something like a true conception of its leading features, it is necessary to test it by comparing it with the statements in contemporary authorities of other countries, and by referring to such earlier native documents as have come down to us. Of the latter class there are only three, and it is requisite that we should form a right conception of their authority. The first are the works of Gildas, who wrote in Latin. They are usually considered as consisting of two pieces, the *Historia* and the *Epistola*, but they may be viewed as forming one treatise. Questions have been raised upon the lives of Gildas, as to whether there was one or two persons of the name—an earlier and a later ; but, viewing the question in its literary aspect, it is of little consequence, for the treatise is evidently the work of one man, and there is evidence in the work itself of his date. The writer states that he was born in the year in which the battle of Badon was fought, and that he wrote forty-four years after.* According to the oldest Welsh annals, the battle of Badon was fought in the year 516, which would place the composition of the treatise in the year 560 ; and the Irish annals record the death of Gildas in 570, ten years after.

Only three MSS. of Gildas are known to have existed, and the oldest of these has since perished. It was in the Cottonian Library (Vit. A. vi.), but fortunately the text of Josseline's edition of Gildas in 1568 was printed from it, and, according to Mr. Petrie, so correctly that it may be taken as representing it.† The other two MSS. are in the public library at Cambridge (Dd, i. 17 and Ff, i. 27)—the one of the end of the fourteenth or beginning of fifteenth centuries, and the other of the thirteenth century. The first is said to have belonged to the monks of Glastonbury, and the second to the monks of Durham. This latter MS. inserts various passages which are not to be found in the other MSS. Thus the other MSS. mention that the Saxons were invited "superbo tyranno," and the Durham MS. inserts the words "Gurthrigerno Britannorum duce." Again, where the

---

* Bede understood this well-known passage as implying that the battle of Badon was fought forty-four years after the arrival of the Saxons ; but it is now generally admitted that this is a mistaken construction of the passage, and that the true import is as above, to which I also give my adhesion.

† Josseline says it had belonged to Christ Church, Canterbury, and was 600 years old.

other MSS. mention the "Obsessio Badonici montis,"
the Durham MS. inserts "qui prope Sabrinum ostium
habetur." The work of Gildas had early found its way
to the Northumbrian monks, as Bede evidently uses it
in his history, and they are probably answerable for
the additions contained in this MS. It has been
remarked that the account given by Gildas of the
departure of the Romans from Britain, and the events
which followed, are inconsistent with the statements of
contemporary Greek and Roman authors; but this
appears to me to arise solely from Gildas having
misplaced the only document directly quoted by him,
which has forced upon his narrative a chronology
inconsistent with the true sequence of events, and
which, unfortunately, has likewise influenced Bede's
history. Gildas narrates two devastations by the
Picts and Scots, after each of which they were driven
back by the Roman troops; then he states the final
departure of the Roman army, followed by the occupation of the territory between the walls by the enemy.
Then he quotes this document, which purports to be a
letter by the Britons, addressed "Actio ter consuli,"
imploring assistance against the "*Barbari*, who drive
them to the sea, while the sea throws them back on the
Barbari." He understands by these "Barbari" the Picts
and Scots, and places after this latter the invitation to
the Saxons, who first drive back the Picts and then unite
with them to subjugate the Britons. Now the exact date
when this letter must have been written can be at once
ascertained, for Aetius was consul for the third time in

446, and the dates of the other events have been fixed in
accordance with this; but while this postdates these
events when compared with the other authorities, the
sequence is the same, with the single exception of the
place occupied by this letter. We know from Zosimus
that the Roman army really left finally in 409. We see,
from Constantius' *Life of St. Germanius* that the
Saxons had already, in alliance with the Picts,
attacked the Britons in 429; and Prosper, a contemporary authority, tells us that in 441 " Britanniæ usque
ad hoc tempus variis cladibus eventibusque latæ, in
ditionem Saxonum rediguntur." It is impossible
to mistake this language. The Saxons must have
completed their conquest six years before the letter
was written, and it follows that the " Barbari " to
which it refers must have meant the Saxons, and that
it was an appeal to the Romans to assist them against
the Saxon invaders. The language of the letter, too,
which seems exaggerated and inapplicable to the
incursions of the Picts and Scots from the north, is
much more natural if directed against the steady and
permanent encroachment of the Saxons from the east.
Take the letter from its present place, and place it
after the narrative of the Saxons turning against the
Britons and attacking them, and the order of events
at once harmonises with the other authorities, while
the necessity for postdating them in Gildas no longer
exists. It was no doubt his misapprehending the
meaning of this document, and misplacing it, which
led to the arrival of the Saxons being supposed to have

taken place after it, and to the date of 447, the succeeding year, being affixed to it by Bede.

The second document is the work usually termed Nennius' *History of the Britons*, and it is very necessary that we should form a right conception of this work, and a correct estimate of its authority. The *Origines*, of Isidorus of Seville, who died in 636, and which must have been compiled some considerable time earlier, soon became widely known, and led to works being written in many countries upon their early history, in which the traditions of the people were engrafted upon it. Either in the same century, or the beginning of the next, a work was compiled in Britain, termed *Historia Britonum*. The author of it is unknown, but the original work appears to have been written in Welsh and translated into Latin. It seems to have acquired popularity at once, and become the basis upon which numerous additions were made from time to time. The original work appears to have belonged more to the North than to Wales, or at least the latter part of it, as the events of that part are mainly connected with the North, and it terminates with the foundation of the Anglic kingdom of Northumbria by Ida. Soon after was added what is termed the *Genealogia*, being the descent of the Saxon kings of the different small kingdoms; but here too Northumbria predominates, and most of the events mentioned in it are connected with its history. It must have been compiled shortly after 738, as that is the latest date to which the history of any of the Saxon kingdoms is brought down; and it too bears the marks of being a translation into Latin from Welsh. An edition of the *Historia* seems to have been made in 823, the fourth year of Mervyn Frych, king of Wales, by Marc the Anchorite, when that part at least of the text which contains portions of the life of Germanus, and probably the legend of St. Patrick, must have been inserted. Another edition in 858 bears the name of Nennius. The original work was very early attributed to Gildas, but latterly the whole work bore the name of Nennius.

The oldest MSS. are of the tenth century, and are three in number. They represent two different editions of the work. The Vatican MS. bears the name of Marc the Anchorite, and contains the date of 946, and the fifth year of King Edmund. It is remarkable enough that this was the year in which that king conquered Cambria, and made it over to Malcolm, king of Scots. It would seem as if this conquest had brought it first under the notice of the Saxons, and this conjecture is further strengthened by the fact that the Paris MS. ex-actly corresponds with this, and that this MS. alone, of all the numerous MSS. which have come down to us, has the names of the Saxon kings in the Saxon and not in the Welsh form.

The MS. which represents the other edition is one in the British Museum (Harl. 3856). It contains in it the date of 796, but there are additions to it not found in any other MS., which must have been compiled in the year 977. These are, *first*, a later chronicle of Welsh

events, from the year 444, and though the last event recorded is in 954, the "anni" have been written down to
977 ; the *second* is a collection of Welsh genealogies,
commencing with that of Owen, son of Howel dda, king
of South Wales, who reigned from 946 to 985,—both in
the paternal and maternal line,—from which we may
infer that the writer was connected with South Wales.
The Chronicle was made the basis of two much later
chronicles, in which the events are brought down to
1286 and 1288, and the whole have been edited under
the name of *Annales Cambriæ*, but the two later
chronicles have in reality no claim to be incorporated
with it, as the differences are not various readings of one
text, but later additions. The great value of this
Chronicle arises from the fact that it was compiled a
century and a half before the Bruts were written, and
it detracts from that value to add to it later additions
taken from chronicles compiled as many years after
the Bruts, and which are obviously derived from them.
It is also the source from which many of the entries
in the Welsh *Brut y Saeson* and *Brut y Tywysogion*
have been translated. It is obvious that both the
Chronicle and the Welsh genealogies were additions
intended to illustrate the *Genealogia* attached to the
Historia. Britonum, and to bring the Welsh history
down to the date of the compiler. The Chronicle inserts the events in the *Genealogia* in the very words
of the latter ; and when the *Genealogia* enumerates
four Welsh kings as fighting against one of the kings
of Bernicia, the Welsh genealogies give the pedigree
of these four kings in the same order.

The *Historia Britonum* was translated into Irish by *Giollacaomhan*, an Irish Sennachy, who died in 1072, and various Irish and Pictish additions were incorporated in the translation.

The work, therefore, as it existed prior to the twelfth century, may be said to consist of six parts : *First*, The original nucleus of the work termed *Historia Britonum; second*, The *Genealogia*, added soon after 738 ; *third*, The *Memorabilia; fourth*, The Legends of St. Germanus and of St. Patrick, added by Marc in 823, the latter being merely attached to his edition, and incorporated in that of Nennius ; *fifth*, The Chronicle and the Welsh genealogies, added in 977 ; and, *sixth*, The Irish and Pictish additions, by Giollacaomhan.* The MSS. of Nennius amount to twenty-eight in number ; and of the later MSS. several seem to have been connected with Durham. To the monks of Durham many interpolations may be traced very similar to those in Gildas : in some MSS. they are written on the margin, and in others incorporated into the text. Thus, when the Mare Fresicum is mentioned, the Durham commentator adds, " quod inter nos Scotosque est." The result of my study of this work is to place its authority higher than is usually done ; and, used with care and with due regard to the alterations made from

---

* The original work will be quoted under the title of the *Historia Britonum*, the second portion under that of the *Genealogia*, or both generally as Nennius, and the fifth as the Chronicle and Genealogies of 977. The Irish Annals will be quoted from the *Chronicles of the Picts and Scots*, recently published, being the first of the series of Scottish Record publications.

time to time, I believe it to contain a valuable summary of early tradition, as well as fragments of real history, which are not to be found elsewhere.

The third native authority prior to the twelfth century is *The Ancient Laws and Institutes of Wales.* They were published by the Record Commission of England in 1841, and the oldest of them, the Laws of Howel dda, are of the tenth century.

Such are the native materials upon which, along with the old Roman and Saxon authorities, any attempt to grasp the leading features of the early history of Wales must be based.

CHAPTER 3.

STATE OF THE COUNTRY IN THE SIXTH CENTURY, AND ITS HISTORY PRIOR TO A.D. 560.

THE state of Wales and the distribution of the Cymric population, between the termination of the Roman dominion and the sixth century, so far as we can gather it from these ancient authorities, does not accord with what we should expect from the ordinary conception of the history of that period, but contrasts in many respects strangely with it.

We are accustomed to regard the Cymric population as occupying Britain south of the wall between the Tyne and the Solway; as exposed to the incursions of the Picts and Scots from the country north of the wall, and inviting the Saxons to protect them from their ravages, who in turn take possession of the south of Britain, and drive the native population gradually back till they are confined to the mountainous region of Wales and to Cornwall. We should expect, therefore, to find Wales the stronghold of the Cymry and exclusively occupied by them; the Saxons in the centre of Britain, and the country north of the wall between the Tyne and Solway surrendered to the barbaric tribes of the Picts and Scots. The picture presented to us, when we can first survey the platform

of these contending races, is something very different.
We find the sea-board of Wales on the west in the
occupation of the *Gwyddyl* or Gael, and the Cymry
confined to the eastern part of Wales only, and placed
between them and the Saxons. A line drawn from
Conway on the north to Swansea on the south would
separate the two races of the Gwyddyl and the Cymry,
on the west and on the east. In North Wales, the
Cymry possessing Powys, with the Gwyddyl in Gwyn-
ned and Mona or Anglesea; in South Wales, the Cymry
possessing Gwent and Morganwg, with the Gwyddyl
in Dyfed ; and Brecknock occupied by the mysterious
Brychan and his family.

On the other hand, from the Dee and the Humber
to the Firths of Forth and Clyde, we find the country
almost entirely possessed by a Cymric population,
where ultimately a powerful Cymric kingdom was
formed ; but this great spread of the Cymric population to the north not entirely unbroken. On the north
of the Solway Firth, between the Nith and Lochryan,
was Galloway with its *Galwydel;* in the centre the
great wood, afterwards forming. the forests of Ettrick
and Selkirk and the district of Tweeddale, extending
from the Ettrick to the range of the Pentland Hills,
and north of that range, stretching to the river Carron,
was the mysterious Manau Gododin with its *Brithwyr.*
On the east coast, from the Tyne to the Esk, settlements of Saxons gradually encroaching on the Cymry.

A very shrewd and sound writer, the Rev. W.
Basil Jones, now Archdeacon of York, struck with this

strange distribution of the population in Wales, has, in his essay, *Vestiges of the Gael in Gwynedd,* revived a theory first suggested by Edward Lhuyd that the Gael preceded the Cymry in the occupation of the whole of Britain, and that these Gael in the western districts of Wales were the remains of the original population, seen, as it were, in the act of departing from the country before the presence of the Cymry; but, though maintained with much ingenuity, it runs counter both to the traditions which indicate their presence and to the real probabilities of the case. Till the year 360 the Roman province extended to the northern wall which crossed the isthmus between the Forth and the Clyde, and the Cymric population was no doubt co-extensive; but in that year barbarian tribes broke into the province, which the Roman authors tell us consisted of the Picts, Scots, and Saxons, and, though driven back, renewed their incursions from time to time. The Saxons, of course, made their descents on the east coast, and Gildas tells us that the Picts came *ab aquilone,* the Scots *a circione,* implying that they came from different directions; while all authorities concur in making Ireland the head-quarters of the latter. The Saxons made their descents on the east coast, the Picts from the north, and the Scots from the west.

Gildas tells us that the Picts finally occupied the country up to the southern wall *pro indigenis,* and settled down in the northern regions; and Nennius, in his account of the arrival of the Scots in Ireland, adds

four settlements of them *in regionibus Britanniæ*,
one of which he expressly says was in Demetia, or
South Wales, and terms the people expelled by
Cunedda and his sons, Scotti. The Scots, therefore,
probably effected a settlement on the west coast of
Wales, as they did on that of Scotland;. and these
foreign settlements in the heart of the Cymric population of Wales and the North seem more probably to
have been permanent deposits remaining from the
frequent incursions of the so-called barbaric tribes on
the Roman province, than vestiges of an original
population.

Relieved from the erroneous chronology applied by
Bede to the events narrated by Gildas, into which he
was led by the false place occupied by the letter to
Aetius, the statements of Gildas harmonise perfectly
with the facts indicated by contemporary Roman and
Greek authors. The barbaric tribes who broke into
the province in 360 were driven back by Theodosius
in 368, and the province restored to the northern
wall. Then follows the usurpation of the title of
Imperator by Maximus in 383, who takes the Roman
troops over to Gaul. This is succeeded by the first
devastatio by the Picts and Scots, when the Britons
apply to the Romans for assistance. Stilicho sends
a single legion, who drive them back and recon-
struct the northern wall. Claudian records the defeat of the barbarian tribes, which he names Picts,
Scots, and Saxons, the fortifying the wall, and the
return of the legion, which was recalled in 402.

Then follows the second *devastatio* by the Picts and
Scots, and the second appeal for assistance, and a
larger force is sent, by whom they are again driven
back. The Roman troops then elect Marcus, after
him Gratian Municeps, and finally Constantine, as
Imperator, who likewise passes over to Gaul with the
troops in 409, after having repaired the southern wall.
Then follows the third *devastatio* by the Picts and Scots,
and Honorius writes to the cities of Britain that they
must protect themselves. The Picts settle down in
the region north of the wall, the Scots return to Ireland, soon to reappear and again effect settlements on
the western sea-board. The Saxons are appealed to
for help, but unite with the Picts to attack the Britons,
and finally bring the greater part of the country under
their subjection in 441, and the Britons vainly appeal
to Aetius for assistance in 446.

Such is a rapid sketch of the events which brought
about the destruction of the Roman province, when
the statements of Gildas are brought into harmony
with those of the classical writers, and which produced
the relative position of the different races presented to
us soon after the final departure of the Romans.

Passing over the legends connected with Gortigern,
as involving an inquiry into his real period and history,
which has no direct bearing upon our immediate
object, and would lead us beyond the limits of this
sketch, the first event that emerges from the darkness which surrounds the British history at this
period, and which influenced the relative position

of the different races constituting its population, is the appearance of Cunedda, his retreat from the north, and the expulsion of the Gael from Wales by his descendants. We are told in the *Historia Britonum* that the Scots who occupied Dyfed and the neighbouring districts of Gower and Cedgueli " expulsi sunt a Cuneda et a filiis ejus ;" and in the *Genealogia* that " Maelcunus Magnus rex apud Brittones regnabat, id est, in regione Guenedote, quia atavus illius, id est, Cunedag, cum filiis suis, quorum numerus octo erat, venerat prius de parte sinistrali, id est, de regione que vocatur Manau Guotodin, centum quadraginta sex annis antequam Mailcun regnaret, et Scottos cum ingentissima clade expulerunt ab istis regionibus." As Mailcun was the first king to reign in Gwynedd after the Scots were driven out, and he was fourth in descent from Cunedda, it is clear that the expression, that they were expelled " a Cuneda cum filiis ejus," is used somewhat loosely, and that the actual expulsion must have been effected by his descendants. In point of fact, we know from other documents that the real agent in the expulsion of the Scots from Gwynedd was Caswallawn Law Hir, the great-grandson of Cunedda and father of Mailcun. If four generations existed between Cunedda and Mailcun, this interval is well enough expressed by a period of 146 years ; but an unfortunate date in the Chronicle of 977 has perplexed the chronology of this period, and led to Cunedda being placed earlier than is necessary. The Chronicle has, under the year 547, " Mortali-

tas magna in qua pausat Mailcun rex Guenedote;"
and if Mailcun died in 547, a period of 146 years
from the beginning of his reign would take us back
to the fourth century, and place Cunedda to-
wards the end of it; but we know from Gildas that
Mailcun did not die in 547, as he was alive and
rapidly rising to power when Gildas wrote in 560, and
the date in the chronicle seems to be a purely artificial date, produced by adding the period 146 years to
the beginning of the century. Gildas mentions that
Maglocunus or Mailcun had, some time previously,
retired into a monastery, from whence he emerged not
long before he wrote, and this is probably the true com-
mencement of his reign. A period of 146 years prior
to 560 brings us to 414; and some years before that
must be considered the true era of the exodus of
Cunedda, with his sons, from Manau Guotodin. It
thus coincides very closely with the period of the occupation of territory between the walls by the Picts on
the final withdrawal of the Roman troops in 409.

Cunedda is termed in all Welsh documents *Guledig*, a name derived from the word *Gulad*, a country,
and signifying Ruler. The same term is applied to
Maximus, who is called in Welsh documents, *Maxim
Guledig*. It is therefore equivalent to the title and
position of Imperator conferred upon him by the
troops in Britain. After Maximus, and before the
Roman troops left Britain, they elected three Imperatores, the last of whom, Constantine, withdrew the
army to Gaul. We know from the *Notitia Imperii*

that the Roman legionary troops were mainly stationed
at the Roman wall and on the Saxon shore, to defend
the province from inroads of the barbarian tribes; and
when the Roman army was finally withdrawn, and
Honorius wrote to the cities of Britain that they must
defend themselves, the Roman troops were probably
replaced by native bodies of warriors, and the functions
of the Roman Imperator continued in the British
Guledig. If this view be correct, the real fact con-
veyed by Nennius' intimation, that Cunedda had left
the regions in the north called Manau Guotodin 146
years before the reign of Mailcun, is that in 410, on the
Picts conquering the land up to the southern wall, the
Guledig had withdrawn from the northern to within the
southern wall.   In the Welsh documents there is also
frequent mention of the *Gosgordd* or retinue in connection with the *Guledig,* which appears to have usually
consisted of 300 horse.   It was certainly a body of men
specially employed in the defence of the borders, as the
Triads of Arthur and his warriors—a document not
subject to the same suspicion as the Historical Triads
—mentions the " three *Gosgordds* of the passes of the
island of Britain," and the *Gosgordd mur* or Gosgordd
of the wall, is also mentioned in the poems.   It seems to
be equivalent to the body of 300 cavalry attached to
the Roman legion ; three times that number, or 900
horse, forming the horse of the auxiliary troops attached
to a legion.

The next *Guledig* mentioned is the notice by
Gildas, in a part of his narrative that indicates a time

somewhat later, that the Britons took arms "duce Ambrosio Auerliano," a man of Roman descent whose relations had borne the purple. The term "Aurelianus" is Gildas' equivalent for *Guledig*, as he afterwards mentions Aurelius Conanus, and both are known in Welsh documents by the names of *Emmrys Guledig* and *Cynan Guledig*; and Ambrosius must have been connected by descent with prior "Imperatores" created by the Roman troops. Gildas then adds that after this "nunc cives, nunc hostes, vincebant usque ad annum obsessionis Badonici montis," and the date of this event is fixed by the chronicle attached to Nennius, which places it in the year 516, in which year Gildas was born.

The period between the success of Ambrosius and the siege of Badon Hill is filled up in the *Historia Britonum* with the account of twelve battles fought by Arthur, of which that of Badon Hill is the last. In the oldest form of the text he is simply termed Arthur, and the title only of "dux bellorum" is given him. It says, "Tunc Arthur pugnabat contra illos (*i.e.* Saxones), in illis diebus cum regibus Britannorum, sed ipse dux erat bellorum." He was not "dux" or "rex Britannorum," but "dux bellorum," a title which plainly indicates the *Guledig*. That he bears here a very different character from the Arthur of romance is plain enough. That the latter was entirely a fictitious person is difficult to believe. There is always some substratum of truth on which the wildest legends are

based, though it may be so disguised and perverted as
hardly to be recognised; and I do not hesitate to receive the Arthur of Nennius as the historic Arthur,
the events recorded of him being not only consistent
with the history of the period, but connected with
localities which can be identified, and with most of
which his name is still associated.   That the events
here recorded of him are not mentioned in the Saxon
Chronicle and other Saxon authorities, is capable of
explanation.   These authorities record the struggle
between the Britons and the Saxons south of the
Humber; but there were settlements of Saxons in the
north even at that early period,* and it is with these
settlements that the war narrated in the *Historia
Britonum* apparently took place.

The *Historia Britonum* records among the various
bodies of Saxons who followed Hengist to Britain one
led by his son Octa and his nephew Ebissa, to whom he
promises " regiones que sunt in aquilone juxta murum
qui vocatur Gual"—the name given by Nennius to the
northern wall.   They arrive with forty ships, and
after ravaging the Orkneys and circumnavigating the
Picts, they occupy " regiones plurimas usque ad con-
finia Pictorum."   The Harleian MS. inserts the words
" ultra Frenessicum Mare," to which the Durham MSS.
add, " quod inter nos Scotosque est," to show that the

---

* I may refer the reader on this subject to my paper on the " Early
Frisian Settlements in Scotland," printed in the *Proceedings of the
Society of Antiquaries* (vol. iv. p. 169).   For the struggle in the south,
the reader cannot do better than refer to Dr. Guest's very able papers
in the *Archæological Journal.*

Firth of Forth is meant. That they may have had settlements beyond the Firth is very probable, but the regions next the wall, as far as the confines of the Picts, can mean nothing but the districts lying between the Forth and Clyde, through which the northern wall passes, as far as the river Forth, which formed at all times the southern boundary of the kingdom of the Picts. These regions are nearly equivalent to the modern counties of Stirling and Dumbarton. All Welsh traditions connected with this war invariably designate Octa and Ebissa, or Eossa as they termed him, and their successors, as Arthur's opponents, and we shall see that the localities of his twelve battles, as recorded by Nennius, are all more or less connected with the districts in the vicinity of the northern wall.

The first battle was " in ostium fluminis quod dicitur Glein." There are two rivers of this name— one in Northumberland, mentioned by Bede as the river where Paulinus baptized the Angles in 627, and the other in Ayrshire. It rises in the mountains which separate that county from Lanarkshire, and falls into the Irvine in the parish of Loudoun. It is more probable that Arthur advanced into Scotland on the west, where he would pass through the friendly country peopled by the Cymry, than through Bernicia, already strongly occupied by bodies of Angles ; and it is at the mouth of the latter river, probably, that he first encountered his opponents. It accords better, too, with the order of his battles, for the second, third, fourth, and fifth, were "super aliud flumen quod dicitur Dubglas et est in regione Linnuis." Here must have been the first severe struggle, as four battles were fought on the same river, and here he must have penetrated the "regiones juxta murum," occupied by the Saxons. Dubglas is the name now called Douglas. There are many rivers and rivulets of this name in Scotland; but none could be said to be "in regione Linnuis," except two rivers—the Upper and Lower Douglas, which fall into Loch Lomond, the one through Glen Douglas, the other at Inveruglas, and are both in the district of the Lennox, the Linnuis of Nennius. Here, no doubt, the great struggle took place, and the hill called Ben Arthur at the head of Loch Long, which towers over this district between the two rivers, perpetuates the name of Arthur in connection with it.

The sixth battle was "super flumen quod vocatur Bassas."[*] There is now no river of this name in Scotland, and it has been supposed to have been somewhere near the Bass Rock, the vicinity of which it is presumed may have given its name to some neighbouring stream. The name Bass, however, is also applied to a peculiar mound having the appearance of being artificial, which is formed near a river, though really formed by natural causes. There is one on the Ury river in Aberdeenshire termed the Bass of Inverury, and there are two on the bank of the Carron, now called Duni-

---

[*] The printed text of the Vatican MS. of Nennius has "Lussas," but this is a mistake. The original MS. reads "Bassas."

pace, erroneously supposed to be formed from the
Gaelic and Latin words *Duni pacis*, or hills of peace,
but the old form of which was *Dunipais*, the latter
syllable being no doubt the same word Bass.   Directly
opposite, the river Bonny flows into the Carron, and
on this river I am disposed to place the sixth battle.

The seventh battle was " in silva Caledonis, id est,
Cat Coit Celidon "—that is, the battle was so called, for
Cat means a battle, and *Coed Celyddon* the Wood of
Celyddon.   This is the Nemus Caledonis that Merlin is
said, in the Latin *Vita Merlini*, to have fled to after the
battle of Ardderyth, and where, according to the tradition
reported by Fordun (B. iii. c. xxvi.), he met Kentigern,
and afterwards was slain by the shepherds of Meldredus,
a regulus of the country on the banks of the Tweed,
" prope oppidum Dunmeller."   Local tradition places
the scene of it in Tweeddale, where, in the parish of
Drumelzier, anciently Dunmeller, in which the name
of Meldredus is preserved, is shown the grave of
Merlin.   The upper part of the valley of the Tweed
was once a great forest, of which the forests of Selkirk
and Ettrick formed a part, and seems to have been
known by the name of the *Coed Celyddon*.

The eighth battle was " in Castello Guinnion."   The
word *castellum* implies a Roman fort, and *Guinnion* is
in Welsh an adjective formed from *gwen*, white.   The
Harleian MS. adds that Arthur carried into battle upon
his shoulders an image of the Virgin Mary, and that the
Pagani were put to flight and a great slaughter made
of them by virtue of the Lord Jesus Christ and of Saint

Mary his mother.   Henry of Huntingdon, who likewise gives this account, says the image was upon his
shield; and it has been well remarked that the Welsh
ysgwyd is a shoulder and *ysgwydd* a shield, and that
a Welsh original had been differently translated.
Another MS. adds that he likewise took into battle
a cross he had brought from Jerusalem, and that the
fragments are still preserved at Wedale.   Wedale is
a district watered by the rivers Gala and Heriot, cor-
responding to the modern parish of Stow, anciently
called the Stow in Wedale.   The name Wedale means
" The dale of woe," and that name having been given
by the Saxons implies that they had experienced
a great disaster here.   The church of Stow being
dedicated to St. Mary, while General Roy places a
Roman castellum not far from it, indicates very
plainly that this was the scene of the battle.

The ninth battle was " in urbe Leogis " according
to the Vatican, " Legionis" according to the Harleian
text.   The former adds " qui Britannice Kairlium
dicitur."   It seems unlikely that a battle could have
been fought at this time with the Saxons at either
Caerleon on the Esk or Caerleon on the Dee, which is
Chester; and these towns Nennius terms in his list not
Kaerlium or Kaerlion, but Kaer Legion.   It is more
probably some town in the north, and the *Memorabilia* of Nennius will afford some indication of the town
intended.   The first of his *Memorabilia* is " Stagnum
Lumonoy," or Loch Lomond, and he adds " non vadit ex
eo ad mare nisi unum flumen quod vocatur Leum "—
that is the Leven.   The Irish Nennius gives the name

correctly *Leamhuin*, and the Ballimote text gives the name of the town, *Cathraig in Leomhan* (for *Leamhan*), the town on the Leven. This was Dumbarton, and the identification is confirmed by the *Bruts*, which place one of Arthur's battles at Alclyd, while his name has been preserved in a parliamentary record of David II. in 1367, which denominates Dumbarton "Castrum Arthuri."

The tenth battle was "in littore fluminis quod vocatur Treuruit." There is much variety in the readings of this name, other MSS. reading it "Trath truiroit," or the shore of Truiroit; but the original Cymric form is given us in two of the poems in the *Black Book:* it is in one *Trywruid*, and in the other *Tratheu Trywruid*. There is no known river bearing a name approaching to this. *Tratheu*, or shores, implies a sea-shore or sandy beach, and can only be applicable to a river having an estuary. An old description of Scotland, written in 1165 by one familiar with Welsh names, says that the river which divides the "regna Anglorum et Scottorum et currit juxta oppidum de Strivelin" was "Scottice vocata *Froch*, Britannice *Werid*."* This Welsh name for the Forth at Stirling has disappeared, but it closely resembles the last part of Nennius' name, and the difference between *wruid*, the last part of the name

---

* *Chronicle of the Picts and Scots*, p. 136.—It may seem strange that I should assert that Gwryd and Forth are the same word. But *Gwr* in Welsh is represented by *Fear* in Irish, the old form of which was *For*, and final *d* in Welsh is in Irish *ch*, in Pictish *th*. The river which falls into the Dee near Bala, in North Wales, is called the Try-weryn, a very similar combination.

Try-wruid, and Werid is trifling. The original form must have been Gwruid or Gwerid, the G disappearing in combination. If by the *traethen Try-wruid* the Links of Forth are meant, and Stirling was the scene of this battle, the name of Arthur is also connected with it by tradition, for William of Worcester, in his *Itinerary,* says "Rex Arthurus custodiebat le round table in castro de Styrlyng aliter Snowdon West Castle."

The eleventh battle was fought "in monte qui dicitur Agned,"—that is in *Mynyd Agned,* or Edinburgh, and here too the name is preserved in *Sedes Arthuri* or Arthur's Seat. This battle seems not to have been fought against the Saxons, for one MS. adds " Cathregonnum," and another " contra illos que nos Cathbregyon appellamus." They were probably Picts.

The twelfth battle was " in Monte Badonis." This is evidently the " obsessio Montes Badonici" of Gildas, and was fought in 516. It has been supposed to have been near Bath, but the resemblance of names seems alone to have led to this tradition. Tradition equally points to the northern Saxons as the opponents, and in Ossa Cyllellaur, who is always named as Arthur's antagonist, there is no doubt that a leader of Octa and Ebissa's Saxons is intended ; while at this date no·conflict between the Britons and the West Saxons could have taken place so far west as Bath. The scene of the battle near Bath was said to be on the Avon, which Layamon mentions as flowing past Badon Hill. But on the Avon, not far from Linlithgow, is a very remarkable hill, of considerable size, the top of which is strongly fortified with double ramparts, and

past which the Avon flows. This hill is called Bouden
Hill. Sibbald says, in his *Account of Linlithgowshire
in* 1710 :—" On the Buden hill are to be seen the vestiges of an outer and inner camp. There is a great
cairn of stones upon Lochcote hills over against Buden,
and in the adjacent ground there have been found
chests of stones with bones in them, but it is uncertain
when or with whom the fight was." As this battle was
the last of twelve which seem to have formed one
series of campaigns, I venture to identify Bouden Hill
with the Mons Badonicus.

According to the view I have taken of the site of
these battles, Arthur's course was first to advance
through the Cymric country, on the west, till he came
to the Glen where he encountered his opponents. He
then invades the regions about the wall, occupied by
the Saxons in the Lennox, where he defeats them in
four battles. He advances along the Strath of the
Carron as far as Dunipace, where, on the Bonny,
his fifth battle is fought; and from thence marches
south through Tweeddale, or the Wood of Celyddon,
fighting a battle by the way, till he comes to the
valley of the Gala, or Wedale, where he defeats the
Saxons of the east coast. He then proceeds to master
four great fortresses : first, *Kaerlium*, or Dumbarton ;
next, Stirling, by defeating the enemy in the *tratheu
Tryweryd*, or Carse of Stirling ; then *Mynyd Agned*,
or Edinburgh, the great stronghold of the Picts, here
called *Cathbregion ;* and, lastly, Boudon Hill, in the
centre of the country, between these strongholds.

The *Bruts* probably relate a fact, in which there is

a basis of real history, when they state that he gave
the districts he had wrested from the Saxons to
three brothers—Urien, Llew, and Arawn. To Urien
he gave Reged, and the district intended by this
name appears from a previous passage, where Arthur
is said to have driven the Picts from Alclyde into
" Mureif, a country which is otherwise termed *Reged*,"
and that they took refuge there in Loch Lomond.
Loch Lomond was therefore in it, and it must have
been the district on the north side of the Roman wall
or *Mur*, from which it was called *Mureif*. To Llew he
gave Lodoneis or Lothian. This district was partly
occupied by the Picts whom Arthur had subdued at
the battle of *Mynyd Agned ;* and this is the Lothus of
the Scotch traditions, who was called King of the
Picts, and whose daughter was the mother of Kentigern. And to Arawn he gave a district which they
call *Yscotlont* or *Prydyn*, and which was probably the
most northern parts of the conquered districts, at least
as far as Stirling.

In 537, twenty-one years after, the Chronicle
of 977 records, " Gweith Camlan in qua Arthur et
Medraut coruere ; " the battle of Camlan, in which
Arthur and Medraut perished. This is the celebrated
battle of Camlan, which figures so largely in the Arthurian romance, where Arthur was said to have
been mortally wounded and carried to Avallon, that
mysterious place ; but here he is simply recorded as
having been killed in battle. It is surprising that
historians should have endeavoured to place this battle
in the south, as the same traditions, which encircle it

with so many fables, indicate very clearly who his antagonists were. Medraut or Modred was the son of that Llew to whom Arthur is said to have given Lothian, and who, as Lothus, King of the Picts, is invariably connected with that part of Scotland. His forces were Saxons, Picts, and Scots, the very races Arthur is said to have conquered in his Scotch campaigns. If it is to be viewed as a real battle at all, it assumes the appearance of an insurrection of the population of these conquered districts, under Medraut, the son of that Llew to whom one of them was given, and we must look for its site there. On the south bank of the Carron, in the very heart of these districts, are remains which have always been regarded as those of an important Roman town, and to this the name of Camelon has long been attached. It has stronger claims than any other to be regarded as the Camlan where Arthur encountered Medraut, with his Picts, Scots, and Saxons, and perished; and its claims are strengthened by the former existence of another ancient building on the opposite side of the river—that singular monument, mentioned as far back as 1293 by the name of " Furnus Arthuri," and subsequently known by that of Arthur's O'on.

In thus endeavouring to identify the localities of these events connected with the names of Cunedda and of Arthur, I do not mean to say that it is all to be accepted as literal history, but as a legendary account of events which had assumed that shape as early as the seventh century, when the text of the *Historia Britonum* was first put together, and which are commemorated in local tradition.

HISTORICAL POEMS CONTAINING ALLUSIONS TO EVENTS PRIOR TO A.D. 560.

A.

POEMS REFERRING TO EARLY TRADITIONS.

I.

THE RECONCILIATION OF LLUD THE LESS.

BOOK OF TALIESSIN LIV.

Notes page 109

IN the name of the God of Trinity, of knowing charity,
A tribe numerous, ungentle their arrogance,
Have overrun Prydain, chief of isles.
Men of the land of Asia, and land of Gafis.
A people of perfect prudence, their country is not known,
Their mother country ; they deviated on account of the sea.
Flowing their coats ; who is like them ?
With discretion let the work of foes be brought about,
Europin, Arafin, Arafanis.
The Christian unmindful was impelled certainly
Before the reconciliation of Llud and Llevelys.
The possessor of the fair isle trembled
Before the chief from Rome, of splendid terror.
Neither hesitating nor crafty the king, fluent his speech.
Who has seen what I have seen of the strange speech ?
There were formed a square mast, the clarions of journey,
Before the presence of Roman leader there is conflagration.

The son of Gradd, of fluent speech, retaliated,
Cymry burning : war on slaves.
20 I will consider, I will deliberate who caused them to go.
The Brythonic energy arose.

II.

THE DEATH-SONG OF CORROI, SON OF DAYRY.

BOOK OF TALIESSIN XLII.

Notes page 109

THY large fountain fills the river,
Thy coming will make thy value of little worth,
The death-song of Corroy agitates me.
If the warrior will allure, rough his temper.
And his evil was greater than its renown was great,
To seize the son of Dayry, lord of the southern sea,
Celebrated was his praise before she was entrusted to him.

Thy large fountain fills the stream.
Thy coming will cause saddling without haste,
The death-song of Corroi is with me now,
If (the warrior) will allure.

Thy large fountain fills the deep.
Thy arrows traverse the strand, not frowning or depressed.
The warrior conquers, great his rank of soldiers,
And after penetrating enters towns
And . . .   the pure stream was promptly whitened.
Whilst the victorious one in the morning heaps carnage ;
Tales will be known to me from sky to earth,
Of the contention of Corroi and Cocholyn,
Numerous their tumults about their borders,

Springs the chief o'er the surrounding mead of the some-
    what gentle wood.
A Caer there was, love-diffusing, not paling, not trembling.
Happy is he whose soul is rewarded.

III.

THE DEATH-SONG OF EROF.

BOOK OF TALIESSIN XL.

Notes page 109

WERE changed the elements
Like night into day,
When came the gloriously-free,
Ercwlf chief of baptism.
Ercwlf said,
That he valued not death.
Shield of the Mordei
Upon him it broke.
Ercwlf the arranger,
Determined, frantic.
Four columns of equal length;
Ruddy gold along them.
The columns of Ercwlf
Will not dare a threatening,
A threatening will not dare.
The heat of the sun did not leave him.
No one went to heaven
Until went he,
Ercwlf the wall-piercer.
May the sand be my covering,
May the Trinity grant me
Mercy on the day of judgment,
In unity without want.

IV.

BOOK OF TALIESSIN XLI.

Notes page 109

MADAWG, the joy of the wall,
Madawg, before he was in the grave,
Was a fortress of abundance
Of games, and society.
The son of Uthyr before he was slain,
From his hand he pledged thee.
Erof the cruel came,
Of impotent joy ;
Of impotent sorrow.
Erof the cruel caused
Treacheries to Jesus.
Though he believed.
The earth quaking,
And the elements darkening,
And a shadow on the world,
And baptism trembling.
An impotent step
Was taken by fierce Erof,
Going in the course of things
Among the hideous fiends
Even to the bottom of Uffern.

V.

BOOK OF TALIESSIN XLVI.

Notes page 110

𝕴 AM Taliesin the ardent;
I will enrich the praise of baptism.
At the baptism of the ruler, the worshipper wondered,
The conflict of the rocks and rocks and plain.
There is trembling from fear of Cunedda the burner,
In Caer Weir and Caer Lliwelydd.
There is trembling from the mutual encounter.
A complete billow of fire over the seas,
A wave in which the brave fell among his companions.
A hundred received his attack on the earth,
Like the roaring of the wind against the ashen spears.
His dogs raised their backs at his presence,
They protected, and believed in his kindness.
The bards are arranged according to accurate canons.
The death of Cunedda, which I deplore, is deplored.
Deplored be the strong protector, the fearless defender,
He will assimilate, he will agree with the deep and shallow,
A deep cutting he will agree to.
(His) discourse raised up the bard stricken in poverty.
Harder against an enemy than a bone.
Pre-eminent is Cunedda before the furrow (*i.c.* the grave)
And the sod. His face was kept
A hundred times before there was dissolution. A door-
    hurdle
The men of Bryniich carried in the battle.
They became pale from fear of him and his terror chill-
    moving.
Before the earth was the portion of his end.

Like a swarm of swift dogs about a thicket.
Sheathing (swords is) a worse cowardice than adversity.
The destiny of an annihilating sleep I deplore,
For the palace, for the shirt of Cunedda ;
For the salt streams, for the freely-dropping sea.
For the prey, and the quantity I lose.
The sarcasm of bards that disparage I will harrow,
And others that thicken I will count.
He was to be admired in the tumult with nine hundred
    horse.
Before the communion of Cunedda,
There would be to me milch cows in summer,
There would be to me a steed in winter,
There would be to me bright wine and oil.
There would be to me a troop of slaves against any advance.
He was diligent of heat from an equally brave visitor.
A chief of lion aspect, ashes become his fellow-countrymen,
Against the son of Edern, before the supremacy of terrors,
He was fierce, dauntless, irresistible,
For the streams of death he is distressed.
He carried the shield in the pre-eminent place,
Truly valiant were his princes.
Sleepiness, and condolence, and pale front,
A good step, will destroy sleep from a believer.

B.

POEMS REFERRING TO ARTHUR THE GULEDIG.

VI.

THE CHAIR OF THE SOVEREIGN.

BOOK OF TALIESSIN XV.

Notes page 110

ᛒᚻᛖHE declaration of a clear song,
Of unbounded Awen,
About a warrior of two authors,
Of the race of the steel Ala.
With his staff and his wisdom,
And his swift irruptions,
And his sovereign prince,
And his scriptural number,
And his red purple,
And his assault over the wall,
And his appropriate chair,
Amongst the retinue of the wall.
Did not (he) lead from Cawrnur
Horses pale supporting burdens?
The sovereign elder.
The generous feeder.
The third deep wise one,
To bless Arthur,
Arthur the blessed,
In a compact song.
On the face in battle,
Upon him a restless activity.
Who are the three chief ministers
That guarded the country?

Who are the three skilful (ones)
That kept the token?
That will come with eagerness
To meet their lord?
High (is) the virtue of·the course,
High will be the gaiety of the old,
High (is) the horn of travelling,
High the kine in the evening.
High (is) truth when it shines,
Higher when it speaks.
High when came from the cauldron
The three awens of Gogyrwen.
I have been Mynawg, wearing a collar,
With a horn in my hand.
He deserves not the chair
That keeps not my word.
With me is the splendid chair,
The inspiration of fluent (and) urgent song.
What the name of the three Caers,
Between the flood and the ebb?
No one knows who is not pressing
The offspring of their president.
Four Caers there are,
In Prydain, stationary,
Chiefs tumultuous.
As for what may not be, it will not be.
It will not be, because it may not be.
Let him be a conductor of fleets.
Let the billow cover over the shingle,
That the land becomes ocean,
So that it leaves not the cliffs,
Nor hill nor dale,
Nor the least of shelter,
Against the wind when it shall rage.

The chair of the sovereign
He that keeps it is skilful.
Let them be sought there!
Let the munificent be sought.
Warriors lost,
I think in a wrathful manner.
From the destruction of chiefs,
In a butchering manner,
From the loricated Legion,
Arose the Guledig,
Around the old renowned boundary.
The sprouting sprigs are broken,
Fragile in like manner.
Fickle and dissolving.
Around the violent borders.
Are the flowing languages.
The briskly-moving stream
Of roving sea-adventurers,
Of the children of Saraphin.
A task deep (and) pure
To liberate Elphin.

VII.

BLACK BOOK OF CAERMARTHEN XXXI.

Notes page 110

WHAT man is the porter?
Glewlwyd Gavaelvawr.
Who is the man that asks it?
Arthur and the fair Cai.
How goes it with thee?
Truly in the best way in the world.
Into my house thou shalt not, come,

Unless thou prevailest.
I forbid it.
Thou shalt see it.
If Wythnaint were to go,
The three would be unlucky :—
Mabon, the son of Mydron,
The servant of Uthir Pendragon ;
Cysgaint, the son of Banon ;
And Gwyn Godybrion.
Terrible were my servants
Defending their rights.
Manawydan, the son of Llyr,
Deep was his counsel.
Did not Manawyd bring
Perforated shields from Trywruid ?
And Mabon, the son of Mellt,
Spotted the grass with blood ?
And Anwas Adeiniog,
And Llwch Llawynnog—
Guardians were they
On Eiddyn Cymminog,
A chieftain that patronised them.
He would have his will and make redress.
Cai entreated him,
While he killed every third person.
When Celli was lost,
Cuelli was found ; and rejoiced
Cai, as long as he hewed down.
Arthur distributed gifts,
The blood trickled down.
In the hall of Awarnach,
Fighting with a hag,
He cleft the head of Palach.
In the fastnesses of Dissethach,

In Mynyd Eiddyn,
He contended with Cynvyn ;
By the hundred there they fell,
There they fell by the hundred,
Before the accomplished Bedwyr.
On the strands of Trywruid,
Contending with Garwlwyd,
Brave was his disposition,
With sword and shield ;
Vanity were the foremost men
Compared with Cai in the battle.
The sword in the battle
Was unerring in his hand.
They were stanch commanders
Of a legion for the benefit of the country—
Bedwyr and Bridlaw ;
Nine hundred would to them listen;
Six hundred gasping for breath
Would be the cost of attacking them.
Servants I have had,
Better it was when they were.
Before the chiefs of Emrais
I saw Cai in haste.
Booty for chieftains
Was Gwrhir among foes ;
Heavy was his vengeance,
Severe his advance.
When he drank from the horn,
He would drink with four.
To battle when he would come
By the hundred would he slaughter;
There was no day that would satisfy him.
Unmerited was the death of Cai.
Cai the fair, and Llachau,

Battles did they sustain,
Before the pang of blue shafts.
In the heights of Ystavingon
Cai pierced nine witches.
Cai the fair went to Mona,
To devastate Llewon.
His shield was ready
Against Cath Palug
When the people welcomed him.
Who pierced the Cath Palug?
Nine score before dawn
Would fall for its food.
Nine score chieftains.

VIII.

BOOK OF TALIESSIN XXX.

Notes page 110

ℑℭ WILL praise the sovereign, supreme king of the land,
Who hath extended his dominion over the shore of the
　　　world.
Complete was the prison of Gweir in Caer Sidi,
Through the spite of Pwyll and Pryderi.
No one before him went into it.
The heavy blue chain held the faithful youth,
And before the spoils of Annwvn woefully he sings,
And till doom shall continue a bard of prayer.
Thrice enough to fill Prydwen, we went into it;
Except seven, none returned from Caer Sidi.

Am I not a candidate for fame, if a song is heard?
In Caer Pedryvan, four its revolutions;
In the first word from the cauldron when spoken,

From the breath of nine maidens it was gently warmed.
Is it not the cauldron of the chief of Annwvn ?   What is
  its intention ?
A ridge about its edge and pearls.
It will not boil the food of a coward, that has not been
  sworn,
A sword bright gleaming to him was raised,
And in the hand of Lleminawg it was left.
And before the door of the gate of Uffern the lamp was
  burning.
And when we went with Arthur, a splendid labour,
Except seven, none returned from Caer Vedwyd.

Am I not a candidate for fame with the listened song
In Caer Pedryvan, in the isle of the strong door ?
The twilight and pitchy darkness were mixed together.
Bright wine their liquor before their retinue.
Thrice enough to fill Prydwen we went on the sea,
Except seven, none returned from Caer Rigor.

I shall not deserve much from the ruler of literature,
Beyond Caer Wydyr they saw not the prowess of Arthur.
Three score Canhwr stood on the wall,
Difficult was a conversation with its sentinel.
Thrice enough to fill Prydwen there went with Arthur,
Except seven, none returned from Caer Golud.

I shall not deserve much from those with long shields.
They know not what day, who the causer,
What hour in the serene day Cwy was born.
Who caused that he should not go to the dales of Devwy.
They know not the brindled ox, thick his head-band.
Seven score knobs in his collar.
And when we went with Arthur of anxious memory,
Except seven, none returned from Caer Vandwy.

I shall not deserve much from those of loose bias,
They know not what day the chief was caused.
What hour in the serene day the owner was born.
What animal they keep, silver its head.
When we went with Arthur of anxious contention,
Except seven, none returned from Caer Ochren.

Monks congregate like dogs in a kennel,
From contact with their superiors they acquire knowledge,
Is one the course of the wind, is one the water of the sea?
Is one the spark of the fire, of unrestrainable tumult?
Monks congregate like wolves,
From contact with their superiors they acquire knowledge.
They know not when the deep night and dawn divide.
Nor what is the course of the wind, or who agitates it,
In what place it dies away, on what land it roars.
The grave of the saint is vanishing from the altar-tomb.
I will pray to the Lord, the great supreme,
That I be not wretched.   Christ be my portion.

IX.

GERAINT, SON OF ERBIN.

BLACK BOOK OF CAERMARTHEN XXII.

Notes page 110

RED BOOK OF HERGEST XIV.

BEFORE Geraint, the enemy of oppression,
I saw white horses jaded and gory,
And after the shout, a terrible resistance.

Before Geraint, the unflinching foe,
I saw horses jaded and gory from the battle,
And after the shout, a terrible impulsion.

Before Geraint, the enemy of tyranny,
I saw horses white with foam,
And after the shout, a terrible torrent.

In Llongborth I saw the rage of slaughter,
And biers beyond all number,
And red-stained men from the assault of Geraint.

In Llongborth I saw the edges of blades in contact,
Men in terror, and blood on the pate,
Before Geraint, the great son of his father.

In Llongborth I saw the spurs
Of men who would not flinch from the dread of the spears,
And the drinking of wine out of the bright glass.

In Llongborth I saw the weapons
Of men, and blood fast dropping,
And after the shout, a fearful return.

In Llongborth I saw Arthur,
And brave men who hewed down with steel,
Emperor, and conductor of the toil.

In Llongborth Geraint was slain,
A brave man from the region of Dyvnaint,
And before they were overpowered, they committed
    slaughter.

Under the thigh of Geraint were swift racers,
Long-legged, with wheat for their corn,
Ruddy ones, with the assault of spotted eagles.

Under the thigh of Geraint were swift racers,
Long their legs, grain was given them,
Ruddy ones, with the assault of black eagles.

Under the thigh of Geraint were swift racers,
Long-legged, restless over their grain,
Ruddy ones, with the assault of red eagles.

Under the thigh of Geraint were swift racers,
Long-legged, grain-scattering,
Ruddy ones, with the assault of white eagles.

Under the thigh of Geraint were swift racers,
Long-legged, with the pace of the stag,
With a nose like that of the consuming fire on a wild
    mountain.

Under the thigh of Geraint were swift racers,
Long-legged, satiated with grain,
Grey ones, with their manes tipped with silver.

Under the thigh of Geraint were swift racers,
Long-legged, well deserving of grain,
Ruddy ones, with the assault of grey eagles.

Under the thigh of Geraint were swift racers,
Long-legged, having corn for food,
Ruddy ones, with the assault of brown eagles.

When Geraint was born, open were the gates of heaven,
Christ granted what was asked,
Beautiful the appearance of glorious Prydain.

C.

POEMS REFERRING TO GWYDYON AP DON AND HIS GWYDDYL AND THE BRITHWYR.

X.

DARONWY.

BOOK OF TALIESSIN X.

Notes page 111

GOD preserve the heavens
From a flood wide spreading.
The first surging billow
Has rolled over the sea-beach.
What tree is greater
Than he, Daronwy ?
I know not for a refuge
Around the proud circle of heaven,
That there is a mystery which is greater.
The light of the men of Goronwy.
Perhaps it may be known,
The magic wand of Mathonwy,
In the wood when it grows.
Fruits more profitable,
On the bank of Gwyllyonwy.
Cynan shall obtain it,
At the time when he governs.
There will come yet
Over the ebb and over the strand,
Four chief sovereignties,
And the fifth not worse.
Men vehement, extensive.

Over Prydain (their) purpose.
Women shall be eloquent,
Strangers shall be captive,
A torrent of longing
For mead and horsemanship.
There will come two ladies,
A widow, and a slender single one ;
Iron their wings,
On warriors brooding.
Chieftains will come,
From about the land of Rome.
Their song will harmonise,
Their praise will spread abroad.
The nature of the oak and thorns
In song will harmonise.
A dog to draw,
A horse to move.
An ox to gore ; a sow to turn up.
The fifth fair young beast Jesus made
From the apparel of Adam to proceed.
The foliage of trees, fair to behold them,
Whilst they were, and whilst it was.
When the Cymry shall commit transgressions,
A foreigner will be found, who will love what was ?
I have leaped a leap from a clear leap,
Good has been dispersed abroad, if a person finds no
      evil.
The funeral-pile of Run, it is an expiation,
Between Caer Rian and Caer Rywg,
Between Dineiddyn and Dineiddwg ;
A clear glance and a watchful sight.
From the agitation of fire smoke will be raised,
And God our Creator will defend us.

XI.

THE PRAISE OF LLUDD THE GREAT.

BOOK OF TALIESSIN LII.

Notes page 111

THE best song they will dispraise,
Eight numbers they will protect,
Monday, they will come,
Devastating they will go.
Tuesday, they will portion
Anger against the adversary.
Wednesday, they will reap.
Pomp in excess.
Thursday, they will part with
The undesired possessor.
Friday, a day of abundance
In the blood of men they will swim.
Saturday　　.　　.　　.
Sunday, certainly,
Assuredly there will come
Five ships and five hundred
That make supplication—

> *O Brithi, Brithi !*
> *Co-occupancy or battle.*
> *Brithi, Brithanai !*
> *Before battle, battle of spears in the field.*

Son of the wood of Cogni,
There will be an adventuring of
Every one to Adonai
On the sward of Pwmpai.
An intimation they prophesy
A long cry against overwhelming,

Long the public harmony
Of Cadwaladyr and Cynan.
The world's profit (is) small,
The heat of the sun is lost.
The Druid will prophesy
What has been will be.
Sky of Geirionydd,
I would go with thee
Gloomy like the evening,
In the recesses of the mountain.
When should be the full length
The Brython in chasing.
To the Brython there will be
Blood of glorious strenuousness,
After gold and golden trinkets.
The devastation of Moni and Lleeni,
And Eryri, a dwelling in it.
It is a perfect prophecy,
With dwellings laid waste.
The Cymry of four languages
Shall change their speech.
Until shall come the cow, the speckled cow
That shall cause a blessing
On a fine day lowing,
On a fine night being boiled,
On the land of the boiler,
In the ships of the consumer.
Let the song of woe be chaunted.
Around the encircling border of Prydain.
They will come, with one purpose,
To resist a maritime disgrace.
Be true the happiness
Of the sovereign of the world.
The worshippers adored together,

To the dale of grievous water it was gone.
A portion full of corn
Invites conflagration.
Without Eppa, without a cow-stall.
Without a luxury of the world.
The world will be desolate, useless.
The deceitful will be fated.
Activity through freshness.
Small men are almost deceived
By the white-bellied trotter.
A hawk upon baptism
The swords of warriors will not pierce Cyllellawr.
They had not what they wished for.
Violent is the grasp of the townman,
And to warriors there is a love of blood.
Cymry, Angles, Gwyddyl, of Prydyn.
The Cymry, swift in mischief,
Will launch their ships on the lake.
The North has been poisoned by rovers
Of a livid hateful hue and form.
Of the race of Adam the ancient.
The third will be brought to set out,
Ravens of the accurate retinue,
The sluggish animals of Seithin.
On sea, an anchor on the Christian.
A cry from the sea, a cry from the mountain,
A cry from the sea, they vigorously utter.
Wood, field, dale, and hill.
Every speech without any one attending,
High minded from every place
There will be confusion.
A multitude enraged,
And distress diffused
Vengeances through ready belief abiding.

That the Creator afflicts, the powerful God of
 exalted state.
A long time before the day of doom.
There will come a day
And a reader will rise,
In the pleasant border of the land of Iwerdon,
To Prydain then will come exaltation,
Brython of the nobility of Rome.
There will be to me a judge unprejudiced, void
 of guile;
The astrologers (or diviners) prophesy,
In the land of the lost ones.
Druids prophesy
Beyond the sea, beyond the Brython.
The summer will not be serene weather,
The noblemen shall be broken,
It will come to them from treachery
Beyond the effusion of the father of Ked.
A thousand in the judgment of exalted Prydain,
And within its united boundary.
May I not fall into the embrace of the swamp,
Into the mob that peoples the depths of Uffern.
I greatly fear the flinty covering
With the Guledig of the boundless country.

XII.

BOOK OF TALIESSIN XIV.

Notes page 111

I WILL adore the love-diffusing Lord of every kindred,
The sovereign of hosts manifestly round the universe.
A battle at the feast over joyless beverage,
A battle against the sons of Llyr in Ebyr Henvelen.

I saw the oppression of the tumult, and wrath and
  tribulation,
The blades gleamed on the glittering helmets,
A battle against the lord of fame, in the dales of the Severn,
Against Brochwel of Powys, that loved my Awen.
A battle in the pleasant course early against Urien,
There falls about our feet blood on destruction.
Shall not my chair be defended from the cauldron of
  Ceridwen ?
May my tongne be free in the sanctuary of the praise of
  Gogyrwen.
The praise of Gogyrwen is an oblation, which has satisfied
Them, with milk, and dew, and acorns.
Let us consider deeply before is heard confession,
That is coming assuredly death nearer and nearer.
And round the lands of Enlli the Dyvi has poured,
Raising the ships on the surface of the plain.
And let us call upon him that hath made us,
That he may protect us from the wrath of the alien nation.
When the isle of Mona shall be called a pleasant field,
Happy they the mild ones, the affliction of the Saxons.
I came to Deganwy to contend
With Maelgwn, the greatest in delinquencies,
I liberated my lord in the presence of the distributor,
Elphin, the sovereign of greatly aspiring ones.
There are to me three chairs regular, accordant,
And until doom they will continue with the singers.
I have been in the battle of Godeu, with Lleu and
  Gwydion,
They changed the form of the elementary trees and sedges.
I have been with Bran in Iwerdon.
I saw when was killed Morddwydtyllon.
I heard a meeting about the minstrels,
With the Gwyddyl, devils, distillers.

From Penryn Wleth to Loch Reon
The Cymry are of one mind, bold heroes.
Deliver thou the Cymry in tribulation.
Three races, cruel from true disposition,
Gwyddyl, and Brython, and Romani,
Create discord and confusion.
And about the boundary of Prydain, beautiful its towns,
There is a battle against chiefs above the mead-vessels,
In the festivals of the Distributor, who bestowed gifts
    upon me.
The chief astrologers received wonderful gifts.
Complete is my chair in Caer Sidi,
No one will be afflicted with disease or old age that may
    be in it.
It is known to Manawyd and Pryderi.
Three utterances, around the fire, will he sing before it,
And around its borders are the streams of the ocean.
And the fruitful fountain is above it,
Is sweeter than white wine the liquor therein.
And when I shall have worshipped thee, Most High,
    before the sod
May I be found in covenant with thee.

XIII.

THE BATTLE OF GODEU.

BOOK OF TALIESSIN VIII.

Notes page 111

𝕴 HAVE been in a multitude of shapes,
Before I assumed a consistent form.
I have been a sword, narrow, variegated,
I will believe when it is apparent.

I have been a tear in the air,
I have been the dullest of stars.
I have been a word among letters,
I have been a book in the origin.
I have been the light of lanterns,
A year and a half.
I have been a continuing bridge,
Over three score Abers.
I have been a course, I have been an eagle.
I have been a coracle in the seas :
I have been compliant in the banquet.
I have been a drop in a shower ;
I have been a sword in the grasp of the hand :
I have been a shield in battle.
I have been a string in a harp,
Disguised for nine years.
In water, in foam.
I have been sponge in the fire,
I have been wood in the covert.
I am not he who will not sing of
A combat though small,
The conflict in the battle of Godeu of sprigs.
Against the Guledig of Prydain,
There passed central horses,
Fleets full of riches.
There passed an animal with wide jaws,
On it there were a hundred heads.
And a battle was contested
Under the root of his tongue ;
And another battle there is
In his *occiput*.
A black sprawling toad,
With a hundred claws on it.
A snake speckled, crested.

A hundred souls through sin
Shall be tormented in its flesh.
I have been in Caer Vevenir,
Thither hastened grass and trees,
Minstrels were singing,
Warrior-bands were wondering,
At the exaltation of the Brython,
That Gwydyon effected.
There was a calling on the Creator,
Upon Christ for causes,
Until when the Eternal
Should deliver those whom he had made.
The Lord answered them,
Through language and elements :
Take the forms of the principal trees,
Arranging yourselves in battle array,
And restraining the public.
Inexperienced in battle hand to hand.
When the trees were enchanted,
In the expectation of not being trees,
The trees uttered their voices
From strings of harmony,
The disputes ceased.
Let us cut short heavy days,
A female restrained the din.
She came forth altogether lovely.
The head of the line, the head was a female.
The advantage of a sleepless cow
Would not make us give way.
The blood of men up to our thighs,
The greatest of importunate mental exertions
Sported in the world.
And one has ended
From considering the deluge,

And Christ crucified,
And the day of judgment near at hand.
The alder-trees, the head of the line,
Formed the van.
The willows and quicken-trees
Came late to the army.
Plum-trees, that are scarce,
Unlonged for of men.
The elaborate medlar-trees,
The objects of contention.
The prickly rose-bushes,
Against a host of giants,
The raspberry brake did
What is better failed
For the security of life.
Privet and woodbine
And ivy on its front,
Like furze to the combat
The cherry-tree was provoked.
The birch, notwithstanding his high mind,
Was late before he was arrayed.
Not because of his cowardice,
But on account of his greatness.
The laburnum held in mind,
That your wild nature was foreign.
Pine-trees in the porch,
The chair of disputation,
By me greatly exalted,
In the presence of kings.
The elm with his retinue,
Did not go aside a foot ;
He would fight with the centre,
And the flanks, and the rear.
Hazel-trees, it was judged

That ample was thy mental exertion.
The privet, happy his lot,
The bull of battle, the lord of the world.
Morawg and Morydd
Were made prosperous in pines.
Holly, it was tinted with green,
He was the hero.
The hawthorn, surrounded by prickles,
With pain at his hand.
The aspen-wood has been topped,
It was topped in battle.
The fern that was plundered.
The broom, in the van of the army,
In the trenches he was hurt.
The gorse did not do well,
Notwithstanding let it overspread.
The heath was victorious, keeping off on all
        sides.
The common people were charmed,
During the proceeding of the men.
The oak, quickly moving,
Before him, tremble heaven and earth.
A valiant door-keeper against an enemy,
His name is considered.
The blue-bells combined,
And caused a consternation.
In rejecting, were rejected,
Others, that were perforated.
Pear-trees, the best intruders
In the conflict of the plain.
A very wrathful wood,
The chestnut is bashful,
The opponent of happiness,
The jet has become black,

The mountain has become crooked,
The woods have become a kiln,
Existing formerly in the great seas,
Since was heard the shout :—
The tops of the birch covered us with leaves,
And transformed us, and changed our faded state.
The branches of the oak have ensnared us
From the Gwarchan of Maelderw.
Laughing on the side of the rock,
The lord is not of an ardent nature.
Not of mother and father,
When I was made,
Did my Creator create me.
Of nine-formed faculties,
Of the fruit of fruits,
Of the fruit of the primordial God,
Of primroses and blossoms of the hill,
Of the flowers of trees and shrubs.
Of earth, of an earthly course,
When I was formed.
Of the flower of nettles,
Of the water of the ninth wave.
I was enchanted by Math,
Before I became immortal,
I was enchanted by Gwydyon
The great purifier of the Brython,
Of Eurwys, of Euron,
Of Euron, of Modron.
Of five battalions of scientific ones,
Teachers, children of Math.
When the removal occurred,
I was enchanted by the Guledig.
When he was half-burnt,
I was enchanted by the sage

Of sages, in the primitive world.
When I had a being ;
When the host of the world was in dignity,
The bard was accustomed to benefits.
To the song of praise I am inclined, which the
    tongue recites.
I played in the twilight,
I slept in purple ;
I was truly in the enchantment
With Dylan, the son of the wave.
In the circumference, in the middle,
Between the knees of kings,
Scattering spears not keen,
From heaven when came,
To the great deep, floods,
In the battle there will be
Four score hundreds,
That will divide according to their will.
They are neither older nor younger,
Than myself in their divisions.
A wonder, Canhwr are born, every one of nine
    hundred.
He was with me also,
With my sword spotted with blood.
Honour was allotted to me
By the Lord, and protection (was) where he was.
If I come to where the boar was killed,
He will compose, he will decompose,
He will form languages.
The strong-handed gleamer, his name,
With a gleam he rules his numbers.
They would spread out in a flame,
When I shall go on high.
I have been a speckled snake on the hill,

I have been a viper in the Llyn.
I have been a bill-hook crooked that cuts,
I have been a ferocious spear
With my chasuble and bowl
I will prophesy not badly,
Four score smokes
On every one what will bring.
Five battalions of arms
Will be caught by my knife.
Six steeds of yellow hue
A hundred times better is
My cream-coloured steed,
Swift as the sea-mew
Which will not pass
Between the sea and the shore.
Am I not pre-eminent in the field of blood?
Over it are a hundred chieftains.
Crimson (is) the gem of my belt,
Gold my shield border.
There has not been born, in the gap,
That has been visiting me,
Except Goronwy,
From the dales of Edrywy.
Long white my fingers,
It is long since I have been a herdsman.
I travelled in the earth,
Before I was a proficient in learning.
I travelled, I made a circuit,
I slept in a hundred islands.
A hundred Caers I have dwelt in.
Ye intelligent Druids,
Declare to Arthur,
What is there more early
Than I that they sing of.

240 And one is come
From considering the deluge,
And Christ crucified,
And the day of future doom.
A golden gem in a golden jewel.
I am splendid
And shall be wanton
From the oppression of the metal-workers.

XIV.

BOOK OF TALIESSIN I.

Notes page 111

RED BOOK OF HERGEST XXIII.

A PRIMITIVE and ingenious address, when thoroughly
    elucidated.
Which was first, is it darkness, is it light?
Or Adam, when he existed, on what day was he created?
Or under the earth's surface, what the foundation?
He who is a legionary will receive no instruction.
Est qui peccator in many things,
Will lose the heavenly country, the community of priests.
In the morning no one comes
If they sing of three spheres.
Angles and Gallwydel,
Let them make their war.
Whence come night and day?
Whence will the eagle become gray?
Whence is it that night is dark?
Whence is it that the linnet is green?
The ebullition of the sea,

How is it not seen?
There are three fountains
In the mountain of roses,
There is a Caer of defence
Under the ocean's wave.
Illusive greeter,
What is the porter's name?
Who was confessor
To the gracious Son of Mary?
What was the most beneficial measure
Which Adam accomplished?
Who will measure Uffern?
How thick its veil?
How wide its mouth?
What the size of its stones?
Or the tops of its whirling trees?
Who bends them so crooked?
Or what fumes may be
About their stems?
Is it Lleu and Gwydyon
That perform their arts?
Or do they know books
When they do?
Whence come night and flood?
How they disappear?
Whither flies night from day;
And how is it not seen?
Pater noster ambulo
Gentis tonans in adjuvando
Sibilem signum
Rogantes fortium.
Excellent in every way around the glens
The two skilful ones make inquiries
About Caer Cerindan Cerindydd

For the draught-horses of pector David.
They have enjoyment—they move about—
May they find me greatly expanding.
The Cymry will be lamenting
While their souls will bé tried
Before a horde of ravagers.
The Cymry, chief wicked ones,
On account of the loss of holy wafers.
There will long be crying and wailing,
And gore will be conspicuous.
There came by sea
The wood-steeds of the strand.
The Angles in council
Shall see signs of
Exultation over Saxons.
The praises of the rulers
Will be celebrated in Sion.
Let the chief builders be
Against the fierce Ffichti,
The Morini Brython.
Their fate has been predicted ;
And the reaping of heroes
About the river Severn.
The stealing is disguised of Ken and Masswy
Ffis amala, ffur, ffir, sel,
Thou wilt discern the Trinity beyond my age
I implore the Creator, hai
Huai, that the Gentile may vanish
From the Gospel   Equally worthy
With the retinue of the wall
Cornu ameni dur.
I have been with skilful men,
With Matheu and Govannon,
With Eunydd and Elestron,

In company with Achwyson,
For a year in Caer Gofannon.
I am old.   I am young.   I am Gwion,
I am universal, I am possessed of penetrating wit.
Thou wilt remember thy old Brython
(And) the Gwyddyl, kiln distillers,
Intoxicating the drunkards.
I am a bard ; I will not disclose secrets to slaves ;
I am a guide : I am expert in contests.
If he would sow, he would plough ; he would plough,
        he would not reap.
If a brother among brothers,
Didactic Bards with swelling breasts will arise
Who will meet around mead-vessels,
And sing wrong poetry
And seek rewards that will not be,
Without law, without regulation, without gifts.
And afterwards will become angry.
There will be commotions and turbulent times,
Seek no peace—it will not accrue to thee.
The Ruler of Heaven knows thy prayer.
From his ardent wrath thy praise has propitiated him
The Sovereign King of Glory addresses me with
        wisdom :—
Hast thou seen the dominus fortis ?
Knowest thou the profound prediction domini ?
To the advantage of Uffern
Hic nemo in por progenie
He has liberated its tumultuous multitude.
Dominus virtutum
Has gathered together those that were in slavery,
And before I existed He had perceived me.
May I be ardently devoted to God !
And before I desire the end of existence,

And before the broken foam shall come upon my lips,
And before I become connected with wooden boards,
May there be festivals to my soul !
Book-learning scarcely tells me
Of severe afflictions after death-bed ;
And such as have heard my bardic books
They shall obtain the region of heaven, the best of
all abodes.

XV.

DEATH-SONG OF DYLAN SON OF THE WAVE.

BOOK OF TALIESSIN XLIII.

Notes page 112

ONE God Supreme, divine, the wisest, the greatest his
habitation,
When he came to the field, who charmed him in the hand of
the extremely liberal.
Or sooner than he, who was on peace on the nature of a turn.
An opposing groom, poison made, a wrathful deed,
Piercing Dylan, a mischievous shore, violence freely flowing.
Wave of Iwerdon, and wave of Manau, and wave of the North,
And wave of Prydain, hosts comely in fours.
I will adore the Father God, the regulator of the country,
without refusing.
The Creator of Heaven, may he admit us into mercy.

XVI.

BLACK BOOK OF CAERMARTHEN XXXV.

Notes page 112

A HORSEMAN resorts to the city,
With his white dogs, and large horns ;
I, who have not before seen thee, know thee not.

A horseman resorts to the river's mouth,
On a stout and warlike steed ;
Come with me, let me not be refused.

I will not go that way at present ;
Bear with the conduct of the delayer ;
And may the blessing of heaven and earth come
    (upon thee).

Thou, who hast not seen me daily,
And who resemblest a prudent man,
How long wilt thou absent thyself, and when wilt
    thou come ?

When I return from Caer Seon,
From contending with Jews,
I will come to the city of Lleu and Gwidion.

Come with me into the city,
Thou shalt have wine which I have set apart,
And pure gold on thy clasp.

I know not the confident man,
Who owns a fire and a couch ;
Fairly and sweetly dost thou speak.

Come with me to my dwelling,
Thou shalt have high foaming wine.
My name is Ugnach, the son of Mydno.

Ugnach ! a blessing on thy throne !
And mayst thou have grace and honour !
I am Taliessin who will repay thee thy banquet.

Taliessin, chief of men,
Victor in the contest of song,
Remain here until Wednesday.

Ugnach! the most affluent in riches,
Grace be to thee from the highest region ;
I will not deserve blame ; I will not tarry.

XVII.

RED BOOK OF HERGEST XXII.

Notes page 112

ЖOW miserable it is to see
Tumult, commotion,
Wounds and confusion,
The Brithwyr in motion,
And a cruel fate.
With the impulse of destiny,
And for heaven's sake
Declare the discontinuance of the disaster !
It is not well that a son should be born :
His youthful destiny
Will necessarily be unbelief
And general privation :—
The Lloegrians declare it.
Alas! for the utter confusion
Until the end of the seventh
From the hard Calends.
True it is, deliverance will come
By means of the wished-for man.
May he throw open the White Mount,
And into Gwynedd make his entry !
The forces of the Cymry

Will be of one course with the lightning :
The signal of their deliverance
Will be a true relief to the bosom :
The guarantee being Reged,
Whose share will be glorious.
Glorious will be our portion.
To me has been given sway,
I have become a predicting bard :
Camlan will be heard again
Scenes of groaning will again be seen,
And dismal lamentations,
And mischievous contention,
And the child will grow
Strong in battle, even when small.
People will see battles,
And the increase of fortresses ;
Many a banner will be shattered :
A red banner I know there is,
It will be death to vanquish it
A signal of their coming,—
The heroic warriors,
Who will defend their fame.
Active their swords before thee,
Before me their virtues.
They shall receive their portion before death.
The day of causing blood-streams,
The day of assailing walls,
Will come for certain,
And fleets on the water,
Neither tax nor tribute
Nor service will succeed,
Nor the entreaties of the weak will avail,
Under the sway of the rulers.
May hens be relics

From Mona to Mynneu!
Believe in the living God for benefits,
Who will dispense us free blessings.
By imploring saints,
And the thorough comprehension of books,
May we obtain, on Thursday, a portion
In the blissful region, the splendid place of rest!

D.

POEM REFERRING TO GWYDDNO AND GWYNN AP NUDD.

XVIII.

BLACK BOOK OF CAERMARTHEN XXXIII.

Notes page 112

A BULL of conflict was he, active in dispersing
    an arrayed army,
The ruler of hosts, indisposed to anger,
Blameless and pure his conduct in protecting life.

Against a hero stout was his advance,
The ruler of hosts, disposer of wrath.
There will be protection for thee since thou askest it.

For thou hast given me protection ;
How warmly wert thou welcomed !
The hero of hosts, from what region thou comest ?

I come from battle and conflict
With a shield in my hand ;
Broken is the helmet by the pushing of spears.

I will address thee, exalted man,
With his shield in distress ;
Brave man, what is thy descent ?

Round-hoofed is my horse, the torment of battle,
Whilst I am called Gwyn, the son of Nud,
The lover of Creurdilad, the daughter of Llud.

Since it is thou, Gwyn, an upright man,
From thee there is no concealing;
I also am Gwydneu Garanhir.

He will not leave me in a parley with thee,
By the bridle, as is becoming;
But will hasten away to his home on the Tawy.

It is not the nearest Tawy I speak of to thee,
But the furthest Tawy;
Eagle! I will cause the furious sea to ebb.

Polishéd is my ring, golden my saddle and bright:
To my sadness
I saw a conflict before Caer Vandwy.

Before Caer Vandwy a host I saw,
Shields were shattered and ribs broken;
Renowned and splendid was he who made the assault.

Gwyn ab Nud, the hope of armies,
Sooner would legions fall before the hoofs
Of thy horses, than broken rushes to the ground.

Handsome my dog and round-bodied,
And truly the best of dogs;
Dormach was he, which belonged to Maelgwn.

Dormach with the ruddy nose! what a gazer
Thou art upon me! because I notice
Thy wanderings on Gwibir Vynyd.

I have been in the place where was killed Gwendoleu,
The son of Ceidaw, the pillar of songs,
When the ravens screamed over blood.

I have been in the place where Bran was killed,
The son of Gweryd, of far-extending fame,
When the ravens of the battle-field screamed.

I have been where Llachau was slain,
The son of Arthur, extolled in songs,
When the ravens screamed over blood.

I have been where Meurig was killed,
The son of Carreian, of honourable fame,
When the ravens screamed over flesh.

I have not been where Gwallawg was killed,
The son of Goholeth, the accomplished,
The resister of Lloegir, the son of Lleynawg.

I have been where the soldiers of Prydain were slain,
From the East to the North;
I am alive, they in their graves!

I have been where the soldiers of Prydain were slain,
From the East to the South
I am alive, they in death!

E.

POEMS REFERRING TO EARLY TRADITIONS WHICH BELONG TO A LATER SCHOOL.

XIX.

THE CHAIR OF CERIDWEN.

BOOK OF TALIESSIN XVI.

Notes page 112

SOVEREIGN of the power of the air, thou also
The satisfaction of my transgressions.
At midnight and at matins
There shone my lights.
Courteous the life of Minawg ap Lleu,
Whom I saw here a short while ago.
The end, in the slope of Lleu.
Ardent was his push in combats ;
Avagddu my son also.
Happy the Lord made him,
In the competition of songs,
His wisdom was better than mine,
The most skilful man ever heard of.
Gwydyon ap Don, of toiling spirits,
Enchanted a woman from blossoms,
And brought pigs from the south.
Since he had no sheltering cots,
Rapid curves, and plaited chains.
He made the forms of horses
From the springing
Plants, and illustrious saddles.
When are judged the chairs,

Excelling them (will be) mine,
My chair, my cauldron, and my laws,
And my pervading eloquence, meet for the chair.
I am called skilful in the court of Don.
I, and Euronwy, and Euron.
I saw a fierce conflict in Nant Frangcon
On a Sunday, at the time of dawn,
Between the bird of wrath and Gwydyon.
Thursday, certainly, they went to Mona
To obtain whirlings and sorcerers.
Arianrod, of laudable aspect, dawn of serenity,
The greatest disgrace evidently on the side of the Brython,
Hastily sends about his court the stream of a rainbow,
A stream that scares away violence from the earth.
The poison of its former state, about the world, it will leave.
They speak not falsely, the books of Beda.
The chair of the Preserver is here.
And till doom, shall continue in Europa.
May the Trinity grant us
Mercy in the day of judgment.
A fair alms from good men.

XX.

THE DEATH-SONG OF UTHYR PENDRAGON.

BOOK OF TALIESSIN XLVIII.

Notes page 112

AM I not with hosts making a din?
I would not cease, between two hosts, without gore.
Am I not he that is called Gorlassar?
My belt was a rainbow to my foe.
Am I not a prince, in darkness,

(To him) that takes my appearance with my two chief
    baskets ?
Am I not, like Cawyl, ploughing ?
I would not cease without gore between two hosts.
Is it not I that will defend my sanctuary ?
In separating with the friends of wrath.
Have I not been accustomed to blood about the wrathful,
A sword-stroke daring against the sons of Cawrnur?
Have I not shared my cause.
A ninth portion in the prowess of Arthur ?
Is it not I that have destroyed a hundred Caers ?
Is it not I that slew a hundred governors ?
Is it not I that have given a hundred veils ?
Is it not I that cut off a hundred heads ?
Is it not I that gave to Heupen
The tremendous sword of the enchanter ?
Is it not I that performed the rights of purification,
When Hayarndor went to the top of the mountain ?
I was bereaved to my sorrow. My confidence was com-
    mensurate.
There was not a world were it not for my progeny.
I am a bard to be praised.   The unskilful
May he be possessed by the ravens and eagle and bird of
    wrath.
Avagddu came to him with his equal,
When the bands of four men feed between two plains,
Abiding in heaven was he, my desire,
Against the eagle, against the fear of the unskilful.
I am a bard, and I am a harper,
I am a piper, and I am a crowder.
Of seven score musicians the very great
Enchanter.   There was of the enamelled honour the
    privilege,
Hu of the expanded wings.

Thy son, thy barded proclamation,
Thy steward, of a gifted father.
My tongue to recite my death-song.
If of stone-work the opposing wall of the world.
May the countenance of Prydain be bright for my guidance,
Sovereign of heaven, let my messages not be rejected.

XXI.

BOOK OF TALIESSIN XLV.

Notes page 112

ⅮISTURBED is the isle of the praise of Hu, the isle
    of the severe recompenser
Mona of the good bowls, of active manliness.   The Menei
    its door.
I have drunk liquor of wine and bragget, from a brother
    departed.
The universal sovereign, the end of every king, the ruinator.
Sorrowful (is) the Dean, since the Archdeacon is interred.
There has not been, there will not be in tribulation his equal.
When Aeddon came from the country of Gwydyon, the
    thickly covered Seon.
A pure poison came four nightly fine-night seasons.
The contemporaries fell, the woods were no shelter against
    the wind on the coast.
Math and Eunyd, skilful with the magic wand, freed the
    elements.
In the life of Gwydyon and Amaethon, there was counsel.
Pierced (is) the front of the shield of the strong, fortunate,
    strong irresistibly.
The powerful combination of his front rank, it was not of
    great account.
Strong (in) feasting ; in every assembly his will was done.

Beloved he went first ; while I am alive, he shall be commemorated.

May I be with Christ, so that I may not be sorrowful, when an apostle,

The generous Archdeacon amongst angels may he be contained.

Disturbed (is) the isle of the praise of Hu, the isle of the severe ruler.

Before the victorious youth, the fortress of the Cymry remained tranquil.

The dragon chief, a rightful proprietor in Britonia.

A sovereign is gone, alas! the chief that is gone to the earth.

Four damsels, after their lamentation, performed their office.

Very grievous truly on sea, without land, long their dwelling.

On account of his integrity (it was) that they were not satiated with distress.

I am blameable if I mention not his good actions.

In the place of Llywy, who shall prohibit, who shall order ?

In the place of Aeddon, who shall support Mona's gentle authorities ?

May I be with Christ, that I may not be sorrowful, for evil or good.

Share of mercy in the country of the governor of perfect life.

XXII.

The Praise of Taliessin.

BOOK OF TALIESSIN XII.

Notes page 116

MESSENGERS to me are come, so numerously are they sent,

We shall bring a mutual conflict, so great is my bosom.

Like the effect of the oar in the brine is the liquor of Beli,

Like a light shield on the back of a shadow.
Like wrath and indignation from the protection
Of a Caer, and nine hundred governors became dead.
There will be a battle on Menei, a vehement retribution.
There will be more on Conwy, the scar of angry strife
    shall cause it.
Cold death the destiny of the ready muse,
From the vehement blade by the stroke of Edyrn.
Three elegant unrestrainable, fell, heavily laden with forces,
There fleets in the stream, an omen of the day of gloom.
Three evenings of battle for three proper
Countries : a boat was made a burying place.
Three of every three : three sins
And Eryri a hill of judgment.
A host of Saxons : the second they were, a third affliction.
In Cymry widowhood awaits women.
Before the presence of Cynan fire broke out.
Cadwaladyr will bewail him.
He injured the country with pain,
Straw ; and roof of houses ; the house he burnt.
There will be a wonder.
A man with the daughter of his brother.
They will cite what is steel
Of the lineage of Anarawd.
From him proceeded
Coch, wise his prudence.
He will not spare nor defend
Either cousin or brother.
At the voice of the warrior's horn,
Nine hundred (were) anxious,
Of universal affliction.
Thou wilt be calling forth verdancy from affected praise,
It will run to such as is oppressed in bosom.

XXIII.

BLACK BOOK OF CAERMARTHEN XXXVIII.

Notes page 116

SEITHENHIN, stand thou forth,
And behold the billowy rows ;
The sea has covered the plain of Gwydneu.

Accursed be the damsel,
Who, after the wailing,
Let loose the Fountain of Venus, the raging deep.

Accursed be the maiden,
Who, after the conflict, let loose
The fountain of Venus, the desolating sea.

A great cry from the roaring sea arises above the
        summit of the rampart,
To-day even to God does the supplication come !
Common after excess there ensues restraint.

A cry from the roaring sea overpowers me this night,
And it is not easy to relieve me ;
Common after excess succeeds adversity.

A cry from the roaring sea comes upon the winds ;
The mighty and beneficent God has caused it !
Common after excess is want.

A cry from the roaring sea
Impels me from my resting-place this night ;
Common after excess is far-extending destruction.

The grave of Seithenhin the weak-minded
Between Caer Cenedir and the shore
Of the great sea and Cinran.

F.

POEMS RELATING TO CITIES OF THE CYMRY AND THEIR LEGENDARY HEROES.

XXIV.

BLACK BOOK OF CAERMARTHEN XV.

Notes page 117

I. DINAS MAON, may God the blessed Sovereign
defend it!
What the sun will dry, Edar will moisten.

II. Dinas Maon, the dislike of Sovereigns, where kings
were hewed down in the obstinate conflict.
What the sun will dry, Mervin will moisten.

III. Dinas Maon, the security of the country, may the
protection of God surround it!
What the sun will dry, Nynaw will moisten.

IV. Mad put his thigh on Merchin the gray steed,
The fort of the brave will defend me.
What the sun will dry, Maelgwn will moisten.

XXV.

BOOK OF TALIESSIN XXI.

Notes page 117

BLACK BOOK OF CAERMARTHEN XIV.

I. I WILL pray God to deliver the people of the fair
(town),
The owner of heaven and earth, all-wise pervader.

A pleasant Caer there is on the surface of the ocean.
May be joyful in the splendid festival its king.
And the time when the sea makes great audacity.
The crowns of bards are usual over mead-vessels.
A wave will come, in haste, speed unto it,
That will bring them to the green sward from the region
    of the Ffichti.
And may I obtain, O God, for my prayer,
When I keep the covenant of conciliation with thee.

A pleasant Caer there is on a broad lake,
A fortress impregnable, the sea surrounds it.
Prydain greets thee : how will these agree?
The point of the lake of the son of Erbin ; be thine the
    oxen.
There has been a retinue, and there has been song, in the
    second place,
And an eagle, high in the sky, and the path of Granwyn,
Before the governing sovereign, that refuses not to start,
The dispersed of renown, and a leader, they form
    themselves.

A pleasant Caer there is on the ninth wave,
Pleasant its denizens in guarding each other.
They will not take them if it be through disgrace.
It is not their custom to be hard.
I will not speak falsely, upon my privilege,
Than the tenants of the two strands better the serfs of
    Dyved,
An associate, if he gives a banquet of deliverers,
Will contain between every two the best multitude.

A pleasant Caer there is, it will be made complete
By meads, and praise, and mountain-birds.

Smooth its songs, on its festival,
And my intelligent Lord, a splendid distributor,
Before he went into his grave, in the boundary of
   the Llan,
He gave me mead and wine from a crystal cup.

A pleasant Caer there is on the shore of the gulf,
Pleasantly is given to every one his share.
I know in Dinbych, white with sea-mews,
A mild associate, the lord of Erlysan.
He was my law, on New Year's eve,
His song (was) solace, the king of splendid war.
And a veil of green colour, and possessing a feast.
This may I be, a tongue over the bards of Prydain.

A pleasant Caer there is, that is supported with gifts,
Mine were its fords, should I have chosen.
I will not speak of the progress of the law that I
   had kept,
He deserves not a New Year's gift that knows not this.
The writing of Prydain, anxious care,
While the waves continue to be agitated about it,
If necessary, far into a cell I would penetrate.

A pleasant Caer there is, rising up,
May we have shares in its meads and praises.
Pleasant on its boundary the sending forth of its
   chieftains.
A cormorant approaches me, long its wings,
There comes to the top of the scream of the sea-birds.
Wrath within fate, let it penetrate the sands and stones,
And the gray wolf the best of conflicts.
May there be derived from above the banquet
   accordant reasonings.

The blessing of the beneficent Ruler of Heaven's
    harmonious heights (be)
Upon them ; may He make denizens (there) the
    worthies of Owain.

A pleasant Caer there is on the margin of the flood.
Pleasantly is given to every (one) his desire.
Address thou Gwyned, be thine the increase.
The dartings of the terrible spears were poured forth.
Wednesday, I saw men in distress,
Thursday, to their disgrace they returned.
And there were crimsoned hair, and clamorous woe.
Exhausted were the men of Gwyned the day that they
    came.
And on Cevn Llech Vaelwy shields they will break.
They fell at the Cevn, a host of kinsmen.

XXVI.

BLACK BOOK OF CAERMARTHEN VIII.

Notes page 117

THE three depredatory horses of the Isle of
    Prydain :—
Carnawlawg, the horse of Owain the son of Urien ;
Bucheslwm Seri, the horse of Gwgawn Gleddyvrudd ;
And Tavawd hir Breich-hir, the horse of Cadwallawn
    the son of Cadvan.

The three draught-horses of the Isle of Prydain :—
Arvul Melyn, the horse of Pasgen the son of Urien ;
Du Hir Terwenydd, the horse of Selyv the son of
    Cynan Garwyn ;
And Drudlwyd, the horse of Rhydderch Hael.

The three spirited horses of the Isle of Prydain :—
Gwineu Goddwf Hir, the horse of Cai ;
Rhuthr Eon Tuth Blaidd, the horse of Gilbert the
    son of Cadgyffro ;
And Ceincaled, the horse of Gwalchmai.

The three high-mettled horses of the Isle of Prydain :—
Lluagor, the horse of Caradawg ;
And Melynlas, the horse of Caswallawn the son of
    Beli.

XXVIII.

BOOK OF TALIESSIN XXV.

Notes page 117

HEAT broke out with matchless fury.
The rapid vehement fire.
Him we praise above the earth,
Fire, the fiery meteor of the dawn.
Above the high gale,
Higher than every cloud.
Great his animal.
He will not delay
Nor the wedding-feast of Llyr.
His path is like a water-course,
Thy rage in the chief streams.
The dawn smiles, repelling gloom,
At the dawn with violence,
At every meet season,
At the meet season of his turnings,
At the four stages of his course,
I will extol him that judges violence,
Of the strong din, deep his wrath.

I am not a man, cowardly, gray,
A scum near the wattle.
The illusion of my two relatives,
Two groans of affliction without appetite.
From my hand to thy hand God will give naught.
Thrice three protections,
Returning to the old places,
With a steed used to the field.
And the steed of Genethawg,
And the steed of Caradawg,
Perfect for travelling.
And the steed of Gwythur,
And the steed of Gwarddur,
And the steed of Arthur.
Dauntless to cause an ache,
And the steed of Taliessin,
And the steed of Lleu half domesticated,
And of Pebyr, the dark gray of the grove.
And Grei, the steed of Cunin.
Cornan stubborn in the conflict,
Of ardent desires,
The Black, from the seas famous,
The steed of Brwyn, betrayer of the country.
And the three cloven-footed ones
They will not go a journey conveniently,
The terrible steed of Ceidaw,
A hoof with bribery on it.
Mottle-shouldered Ysgodig
The steed of Llemenig
The horse of Rhydderch Rhyddig
Of the gray colour of a pear.
And Llamre, full of inherent vigour,
And Froenvoll of a vigorous growth,
The steed of Sadyrnin,

And the steed of Constantine.
And others handling,
For the country, the smart of foreigners.
The good Henwyn brought
A tale from Hiraddug.
I have been a sow, I have been a buck,
I have been a sage, I have been a snout,
I have been a horn, I have been a wild sow,
I have been a shout in battle.
I have been a torrent on the slope,
I have been a wave on the extended shore.
I have been the light sprinkling of a deluge,
I have been a cat with a speckled head on three trees.
I have been a circumference, I have been a head.
A goat on an elder-tree.
I have been a crane well filled, a sight to behold.
Very ardent the animals of Morial,
They kept a good stock.
Of what is below the air, say the hateful men,
Too many do not live, of those that know me.

XXIX.

THE VERSES OF THE GRAVES.

BLACK BOOK OF CAERMARTHEN XIX.

Notes page 117

THE graves which the rain bedews?
Men that were not accustomed to afflict me :—
Cerwyd, and Cywryd, and Caw.

The graves which the thicket covers?
They would not succumb without avenging themselves :
Gwryen, Morien, and Morial.

The graves which the shower bedews ?
Men that would not succumb stealthily :—
Gwen, and Gwrien, and Gwriad.

The grave of Tydain, father of the Muse, in the
      region of Bron Aren :
Where the wave makes a sullen sound
The grave of Dylan in Llan Beuno.

The grave of Ceri Gledyvhir, in the region of Hen
      Eglwys,
In a rugged steep place ;
Tarw Torment in the enclosure of Corbre.

The grave of Seithenhin the weak-minded
Between Caer Cenedir and the shore
Of the great sea and Cinran.

In Aber Gwenoli is the grave of Pryderi,
Where the waves beat against the land ;
In Carrawg is the grave of Gwallawg Hir.

The grave of Gwalchmai is in Peryddon,
Where the ninth wave flows :
The grave of Cynon is in Llan Badarn.

The grave of Gwrwawd the honourable is
In a lofty region : in a lowly place of repose,
The grave of Cynon the son of Clydno Eiddyn.

The grave of Run the son of Pyd is by the river
      Ergryd,
In a cold place in the earth.
The grave of Cynon is in Ryd Reon.

Whose is the grave beneath the hill?
The grave of a man mighty in the conflict—
The grave of Cynon the son of Clydno Eiddyn.

The grave of the son of Osvran is in Camlan,
After many a slaughter
The grave of Bedwyr is in Gallt Tryvan.

The grave of Owain ab Urien in a secluded part of
    the world,
Under the sod of Llan Morvael;
In Abererch, that of Rhydderch Hael.

After wearing dark-brown clothes, and red, and
    splendid,
And riding magnificent steeds with sharp spears,
In Llan Heledd is the grave of Owain.

After wounds and bloody plains,
And wearing harness and riding white horses,
This, even this, is the grave of Cynddylan.

Who owns the grave of good connections?
He who would attack Lloegir of the compact host—
The grave of Gwen, the son of Llywarch Hen, is this.

Whose is the grave in the circular space,
Which is covered by the sea and the border of the valley?
The grave of Meigen, the son of Run, the ruler of a
    hundred.

Whose is the grave in the island,
Which is covered by the sea with a border of tumult?
The grave of Meigen, the son of Run, the ruler of a court

Narrow is the grave and long,
With respect to many long every way :—
The grave of Meigen, the son of Run, the ruler of right.

The grave of the three serene persons on an elevated hill,
In the valley of Gwynn Gwynionawg—
Mor, and Meilyr, and Madawg.

The grave of Madawg, the splendid bulwark
In the meeting of contention, the grandson of Urien,
The best son to Gwyn of Gwynlliwg.

The grave of Mor, the magnificent, immovable sovereign,
The foremost pillar in the conflict,
The son of Peredur Penwedig.

. The grave of Meilyr Malwynawg of a sullenly-disposed
        mind.
The hastener of a fortunate career,
Son to Brwyn of Brycheinawg.

Whose is the grave in Ryd Vaen Ced
With its head in a downward direction ?
The grave of Run, the son of Alun Dywed.

The grave of Alun Dywed in his own region,
Away he would not retreat from a difficulty—
The son of Meigen, it was well when he was born.

The grave of Llia the Gwyddel is in the retreat of
        Ardudwy,
Under the grass and withered leaves ;
The grave of Epynt is in the vale of Gewel.

The Grave of Dywel, the son of Erbin, is in the plain
    of Caeaw ;
He would not be a vassal to a king ;
Blameless, he would not shrink from battle.

The Grave of Gwrgi, a hero and a Gwyndodian lion ;
And the grave of Llawr, the regulator of hosts.
In the upper part of Gwanas the men are !

The long graves in Gwanas—
Their history is not had,
Whose they are and what their deeds.

There has been the family of Oeth and Anoeth—
Naked are their men and their youth—
Let him who seeks for them dig in Gwanas.

The grave of Llwch Llawengin is on the river
    Cerddenin,
The head of the Saxons of the district of Erbin ;
He would not be three months without a battle.

The graves in the Long Mountain—
Multitudes well know it—
Are the graves of Gwryen, Gwryd Engwawd, and
    Llwyddawg the son of Lliwelydd.

Who owns the grave in the mountain ?
One who marshalled armies—
It is the grave of Ffyrnvael Hael, the son of Hyvlydd.

Whose grave is this ? The grave of Eiddiwlch the
    Tall,
In the upland of Pennant Twrch,
The son of Arthan, accustomed to slaughter.

The grave of Llew Llawgyffes under the protection
    of the sea,
With which he was familiar ;
He was a man that never gave the truth to any one.

The grave of Beidawg the Ruddy in the vicinity of
    Riw Llyvnaw ;
The grave of Lluosgar in Ceri ;
And at Ryd Bridw the grave of Omni.

Far his turmoil and his seclusion ;
The sod of Machawe conceals him ;
Long the lamentations for the prowess of Beidawg
    the Ruddy.

Far his turmoil and his fame—
The sod of Machawe is upon him—
This is Beidawg the Ruddy, the son of Emyr Llydaw.

The grave of a monarch of Prydain is in Lleudir
    Gwynasedd,
Where the flood enters the Llychwr ;
In Celli Briafael, the grave of Gyrthmwl.

The grave in Ystyvachau,
Which everybody doubts.
The grave of Gwrtheyrn Gwrthenau.

Cian wails in the waste of Cnud,
Yonder above the grave of the stranger—
The grave of Cynddilig, the son of Corcnud.

Truly did Elffin bring me
To try my primitive bardic lore

Over a chieftain—
The grave of Rwvawn with the imperious aspect.

Truly did Elffin bring me
To try my bardic lore
Over an early chieftain—
The grave of Rwvawn, too early gone to the grave.

The grave of March, the grave of Gwythur,
The grave of Gwgawn Gleddyvrudd ;
A mystery to the world, the grave of Arthur.

The grave of Elchwith is by the rain bedewed,
With the plain of Meweddawg under it ;
Cynon ought to bewail him there.

Who owns this grave? this grave? and this?
Ask me, I know it ;
The grave of Ew, the grave of Eddew was this,
And the grave of Eidal with the lofty mien.

Eiddew and Eidal, the unflinching exiles,
The whelps of Cylchwydrai :
The sons of Meigen bred war-horses.

Whose is this grave? It is the grave of Brwyno
        the Tall,
Bold were his men in his region.
Where he would be, there would be no flight.

Who owns this grave—not another?
Gwythwch, the vehement in the conflict,
While he would kill thee, he would at thee laugh.

The grave of Silid the intrepid is in the locality of
    Edrywfy ;
The grave of Llemenig in Llan Elwy,
In the swampy upland is the grave of Eilinwy.

The grave of a stately warrior ; many a carcase
Was usual from his hand,
Before he became silent beneath the stones ;
Llachar, the son of Run, is in the valley of the Cain.

The grave of Talan Talyrth
Is at the contention of three battles,
A hewer down of the head of every force,
Liberal was he, and open his gates.

The grave of Elisner, the son of Ner,
Is in the depth of the earth without fear, without
    concern ;
A commander of hosts was he, so long as his time
    lasted.

The grave of a hero vehement in his rage
Llachar the ruler of hosts, at the confluence of noisy
    waters,
Where the Tawne forms a wave.

Whose are graves in the fords ?
What is the grave of a chieftain, the son of Rygenau,
A man whose arms had abundant success.

Whose is this grave ? The grave of Braint
Between Llewin and Llednaint—
The grave of a man, the woe of his foes.

Whose is the grave on the slope of the hill ?
Many who know it do not ask ;
The grave of Coel, the son of Cynvelyn.

The grave of Dehewaint is on the river Clewaint,
In the uplands of Mathavarn,
The support of mighty warriors.

The grave of Aron, the son of Dewinvin, is in the
    land of Gwenle ;
He would not shout after thieves,
Nor disclose the truth to enemies.

The grave of Tavlogau, the son of Ludd,
Is far away in Trewrudd ; and thus to us there is
    affliction ;
He who buried him obtained an advantage.

Who owns the grave on the banks of Ryddnant ?
Run his name, his bounties were infinite ;
A chief he was ! Riogan pierced him.

He was like Cyvnyssen to demand satisfaction for
    murder,
Ruddy was his lance, serene his aspect :
Who derived the benefit ? The grave of Bradwen.

Whose is the quadrangular grave
With its four stones around the front?
The grave of Madawg the intrepid warrior.

In the soil of the region of Eivionydd,
There is a tall man of fine growth,
Who would kill all when he was greatly enraged.

The three graves on the ridge of Celvi,
The Awen has declared them to me :—
The grave of Cynon of the rugged brows,
The grave of Cynvael, and the grave of Cynveli.

The grave of Llwid Llednais in the land of Cemmaes,
Before his ribs had grown long,
The bull of conflict brought oppression thither.

The grave of the stately Siawn in Hirerw,
A mountain between the plain and the oaken forest,
Laughing, treacherous, and of bitter disposition was he.

Who owns the grave in the sheltered place?
While he was, he was no weakling :—
It is the grave of Ebediw, the son of Maelur.

Whose is the grave in yonder woody cliff?
His hand was an enemy to many ;—
The bull of battle—mercy to him !

The graves of the sea-marsh.
Slightly are they ornamented !
There is Sanawg, a stately maid ;
There is Run, ardent in war;
There is Earwen, the daughter of Hennin ;
There are Lledin and Llywy.

The grave of Hennin Henben is in the heart of
        Dinorben ;
The grave of Aergwl in Dyved,
At the ford of Cynan Gyhored.

Every one that is not dilatory inquires—
Whose is the mausoleum that is here?
It is the grave of Einyawn, the son of Cunedda ;
It is a disgrace that in Prydain he should have been
        slain.

Who owns the grave in the great plain?
Proud his hand upon his lance :—
The grave of Beli, the son of Benlli Gawr.

NOTES ON THE POEMS

(For the original Welsh text, see vol. 2 of Skene's Four Ancient Books of Wales; for a modern Welsh text of the Book of Taliesin, see Sir Ifor Williams' The Poems of Taliesin, with English explanatory notes by J. E. C. Williams, Dublin Institute for Advanced Studies, 1975).

I. The Reconciliation of Llud the Less. Llud and Llevelys occur in surviving Welsh legends as two brothers living in perfect harmony. This poem must refer to the end of a quarrel between them, the legend of which has been lost.

II. The Death-Song of Carroi, Son of Dayry. This is a Welsh poem about an Irish hero of the Ulster cycle, Curoi mac Dairi. Although Skene considered this to be an early composition, Sir Ifor Williams thought that it had been composed later, somewhere between 900 and 1100.

III. The Death-Song of Erof. Erof does not occur in this poem, but in the next one; it is likely that a mediaeval scribe wrote the title of the next poem here, out of place. This poem, in fact, refers to Ercwlf (Hercules) and his columns or pillars!

IV. The reference to the wall in the first line probably links this poem with the post-Roman period when the Britons had to defend themselves against the barbarians from the North. We know little about Madawg, but he may have been well known in mediaeval Wales; he is described as 'son of Uthyr,' and must have been Arthur's brother, or half-brother. Erof is said to be Welsh for Herod.

V. This is an elegy on Cunedda, who is said to have returned from the North to Wales, where he and his sons or descendants drove out the Scots, or Gwyddyl, returning the land to the Cymry.

VI. The Chair of the Sovereign. Skene thought that the reference to a 'warrior of two authors' meant the Guledig. Ala was the name of a troop of horse in the Roman army. The reference to an 'assault on the wall' implies that this poem also belongs to the time when the Britons were defending the northern wall themselves. The poem also mentions Prydain or the land of the South Cymry.

VII. This poem mentions Arthur and Cai, and the reference to Mynyd Eiddyn or Edinburg links it with Scotland. A number of Scottish legends make reference to nine women of one sort or another, and here we find Cai piercing 'nine witches.'

VIII. This poem is usually called the Spoils of Annwn. It is about a raid on the Celtic otherworld, aimed at stealing a magic cauldron. Arthur sails there in his ship Prydwen with three times its normal complement, but only seven of them return alive. Here we can no longer think of Arthur as the historical Guledig, for he has been given a role in Celtic mythology, perhaps supplanting an earlier hero. For a discussion of this poem, see the book by R. S. Loomis, 'Wales and the Arthurian Legend,' Univ. of Wales Press, 1956.

IX. Geraint, son of Erbin. This elegy on Geraint is to be found in the Black Book of Carmarthen, and also in the Red Book of Hergest. It has been attributed to Llwyarch Hen.

X. Daronwy. Sir Ifor Williams links this poem with Anglesey, where there is still a house bearing the name. The first part refers to Prydain, Wales, but near the end there is mention of Dineiddyn, implying a Scottish link.

Skene placed this poem, and the seven which follow it, as referring to 'Gwydyon ap Don and his Gwyddyl and the Brithwyr.' The Gwyddyl are the Scots from Ireland who had settled in the West; the Brithwyr are the Picts; Gwydyon ap Don, or Gwydion son of Don, figures in Welsh mythology as a magician. Don is the Welsh equivalent of the mother-goddess Danu of the Irish divine pantheon.

XI. Skene thought that this poem referred to the Gwyddyl of Gwydyon ap Don. The mention of 'Cymry, Angles, Gwyddyl of Prydyn,' links this poem with events in Scotland, possibly with the time when many of the North Cymry lapsed from Christianity, formed an alliance with their neighbours, and rebelled against the South.

XII. The reference to the war between Brochwel of Powys and Ethelfrith means that this poem could not have been composed before 613.

XIII. The Battle of Godeu. This poem mentions a war 'against the Guledig of Prydain.' The Picts or Brithwyr (speckled men) are described as 'a snake speckled.' This poem seems to refer to the rebellious alliance of the Northern Cymry with the Picts and Scots; it also mentions Arthur. Sir Ifor Williams has, however, posed the question: what about the Battle of Celyddon Wood? because Goddau means trees!

XIV. Skene thought this also had Scottish links.

XV. Iwerdon is Ireland, Manau the Isle of Man, Y Gogledd is Prydyn (Scotland/Cumbria), Prydain is the land of the South Cymry (Wales &c.).

XVI. This poem is a dialogue between Taliesin and Ugnach. Caer Sion means the Fort of Zion, or Jeruselem.

XVII. The Brithwyr are the Picts, the Leogrians the English. There is mention of Gwynedd in North Wales, and of Reged, one of the kingdoms of the northern Cymry. There is also a mention of the Battle of Camlan.

XVIII. This poem takes the form of a dialogue between Gwyn ap Nud and Gwyddneu Geranhir. The latter figures historically amongst the 'Men of the North,' and also as a mythological character. In Welsh folk-lore, Gwyn ap Nud was lord of the otherworld; it is said that he had a palace on top of Glastonbury Tor.

XIX. The Chair of Ceredwen. This poem refers to events in the Mabinogi, which none of the early ones do; it mentions the books of Beda (Bede) and therefore it must have been composed after 735.

XX. The Death-Song of Uthyr Pendragon. Uthyr was Arthur's father. Skene was of the opinion that this poem was composed in South Wales in imitation of those truly ancient poems associated with the name of Taliesin.

XXI. Skene thought this one had been composed between 1380 and 1420, but Sir Ifor Williams put it in the eleventh century, possibly the first half of the latter, for there is no reference to the

Normans. It is probably based on a much older poem, and it refers to Anglesey - Mona, - and Menei. It is a confusing poem, and one which Sir Ifor Williams thought had been badly translated in Skene; therefore we give it a longer note:

The basic theme is one of praise of a lord of Anglesey, who has just died. Something bad has happened in the dead of night, possibly the arrival of the four damsels mentioned later, whom the poet criticizes for not having been distressed by their lord's death. Sir Ifor has given a modern literal translation of this poem in The Beginnings of Welsh Poetry, adding that the reader can use his or her own imagination to fill in the gaps, or fall back on the one in Skene. He has pointed out that the version in Skene requires the following corrections: (1) 'Isle of the praise of Hu' is taken from 'huynys' which is an unknown word in Welsh; it could be a mis-spelling of 'huenys,' meaning splended or glorious, so that Island splended in song, or praise, would be a more correct rendering. (2) 'Four nightly fine-night seasons' is not clear, and the literal meaning is 'four bare-headed in the dead of night,' possibly the arrival of the four damsels. (3) 'May I be with Christ, so that I may not be sorrowful when an apostle' is not logical; it may be better rendered by 'may I receive from Christ an apostle's share, that I may not be sad.' (4) The lord is given the name of Aeddon, but this may simply mean 'lord,' and this would make sense of 'archaeddon,' or arch-lord in the Welsh text, which is wrongly translated as Archdeacon in Skene's version.

As an alternative to our version from Skene, we give overleaf the little-known translation by Stephens (from the appendix to The Gododin of Aneurin):

The Elegy of Aeddon of Mona.

I

Terrible island!
Boldly praised island
  Of the severe rewarder!
Mona! (land of) charming cuckoos,
Of the manliness of Ervei;
  Menei is its portal
(There) I drank liquor,
Wine and Braggett,
  With a brother - now departed.
The universal ruler,
The end of all emulation,
  The ruinator of sovereignty,
Rueful destiny!
Demanded Aeddon,
  For the grave.
There has not been,
There will not be, his equal
  In tribulation.
When Aeddon came
From the land of Gwydion,
  The strong door of Seon,
He was an acute afflictor;
In four nocturnal (attacks),
  In the serene season,
His contemporaries fell;
The words afforded no protection,
  The wind was on their skirts,
Math and Eunydd*,
Skilful with the magic wand,
  Set the elements at large;

*This is Math ap Mathonwy, a celebrated character in Welsh
romance, who was considered to have excelled all in his
power of enchantment. Eunydd, also an enchanter, was the
brother of Gwydion ap Don.

In the time of Gwydion
And Amaethon*,
  There was counsel.
Pierced was the front of his shield;
He was strong and fortunate,
  Strong and irresistible.
He was mighty in the carouse;
In every congress
  His will was done.
Kind forerunner,
While I am living,
  He shall be celebrated.
The powerful combination
Of his front rank
  Was not serviceable (to his enemies).
[May I be with Christ (i.e. dead),
If I am not sorrowful,
  That the generous apostle,
  Demanded Aeddon,
To be contained
  Among the angels].
                    II
Terrible island!
Boldly praised island
  Of the ardent ruler!
In the presence of the victor youth,
The fortress of the Kymry
  Remained tranquil.

---

*Gwydion and Amaethon belonged to the Gaelic settlers (or
Gwyddyl) in Anglesey. (We have already noted the demigod
status of Gwydion son of Don, in Welsh mythology. One of
the problems with many of these old poems, is that historical
characters bear the same names as the gods, demigods and
heroes of mythology, and it is not always clear to which the
poet is alluding. In this particular case, of course, the reference is clearly to the historical Gwydion - editor).

The dragon chief,
Was a rightful owner
    In Britannia;
Consuming dominator,
Lord of a coast
    Facing land!
Four damsels,
After their lamentation,
    Will suffer misery.
In affliction dire,
On sea without land,
    Tedious will be their existence.
On account of his integrity,
There is no cessation
    Of their sorrow.
I am blameable
That I do not mention
    The good he did to me.
For the impetuous paragon,
Who will prohibit,
    Who will put in order?
For the impetuous Aeddon,
What benign associate
    Will support Mon?
[May I be with Christ,
If I am not sorrowful
    For the evil, of the good
Share of mercy,
In the land of renown
    And perfect life.]

XXII. The praise of Taliesin. This poem includes a reference to Anarawd, who was the son of Rhodri Mawr. The latter died in 913.

XXIII. This poem is attributed to Gwyddnew or Gwyddno who was both prince and poet. He is said to have composed it when the sea overcame low-lying land in Cardigan Bay, because, says the legend, a drunkard had left the sluice gates open. There are many Celtic tales of lands lost beneath the sea. This one is reminiscent of Albert the Great's story of the engulfing of the City of Is, off the coast of Brittany.

XXIV. Dinas Maon - the City of the People.

XXV. A poem in praise of Tenby (Dinbych). Sir Ifor Williams points out that although there is no official recognition of an early settlement at Tenby, this is not surprising, as the building of a castle on the site would have removed all trace of former earthworks and wooden structures. The oldest records show Tenby as a Viking settlement called Tembych, but the Vikings may have taken the name from the older Welsh one of Dinbych. For an expanded discussion of this poem, see 'The Beginnings of Welsh Poetry' (op. cit.).

XXVI. This is not really a poem, but triads about famous horses.

XXVII. This is missing, probably a mistake in numbering in the preparation of Skene's book.

XXVIII. This one is included because it refers to famous horses, and links with the previous one.

XXIX. This poem is also known as the Verses of the Warriors Graves; it speaks of past heroes, known and unknown.

ALSO PUBLISHED BY LLANERCH:

The Mystical Way and the Arthurian Quest
By Derek Bryce. ISBN 0947992073

Celtic Folk-Tales From Armorica
By F. M. Luzel. ISBN 0947992049

The Celtic Legend Of The Beyond
By Anatole Le Braz. ISBN 0947992065

From Booksellers,
or by mail-order
from the publishers.
Write for a current price list
for these, and other books.
Llanerch Enterprises,
Felinfach, Lampeter,
Dyfed, Wales. SA48 8PJ.

Printed
on
vellum
cartridge
in a run
of only
450
copies